1994 Guide to INCOME TAX

REVISED AND UPDATED EDITION

PREPARED BY
David B. Genders, F.C.A.
A partner in Sayers Butterworth, Chartered Accountants

HarperCollins*Publishers*

HarperCollins Publishers
P.O. Box, Glasgow G4 0NB

All rights reserved. No part of this publication may be reproduced, stored in a retrieval system or transmitted, in any form or by any means, electronic, mechanical, photocopying, recording or otherwise, without the prior permission of the publisher.

This book is sold subject to the conditions that it shall not, by way of trade or otherwise, be lent, re-sold, hired out or otherwise circulated without the publisher's prior consent in any form of binding or cover other than that in which it is published and without a similar condition including this condition being imposed on the subsequent purchaser.

First published 1974
18th edition, completely revised and reset 1994.

© Daily Telegraph 1974, 1994

ISBN 0 00 470558 0

Printed in Great Britain by HarperCollins Manufacturing, Glasgow

ACKNOWLEDGEMENT

The Inland Revenue forms reproduced in this book are Crown copyright and are reproduced with the permission of the Controller of Her Majesty's Stationery Office.

CONTENTS

	Introduction	v
1	**How the Tax System Works**	1
	The Inspector of Taxes, The Collector of Taxes, Communicating with the Inland Revenue, The Taxpayer's Charter, Complaints, Changes in legislation, Income Tax rates for 1993/94	
2	**Personal Allowances and Reliefs**	7
	Personal allowance, Married couple's allowance, Age allowances, Additional personal allowance, Widow's bereavement allowance, Blind person's relief, Transfer of allowances, Relief on life assurance premiums	
3	**Interest Payments and Other Outgoings**	18
	Your own home, A home for a dependent relative, Let property, Business loans, Charitable deeds of covenant, Gift Aid, Payroll deduction scheme, Private medical insurance, Vocational training	
4	**Earnings from Employment**	25
	Code numbers, The assessment, Changing your job, Expenses, Employee share ownership, Profit-related pay, Payments on termination of employment, National Insurance	
5	**Value Added Tax**	39
	Rates of tax, Registration, Records and accounting, Input tax, Special schemes for retailers, Helpful schemes for smaller businesses, Partial exemption, Control visits, Penalties, surcharges and interest, Appeals, Local VAT offices, Supplies to/from EC countries	
6	**The Self-Employed**	48
	Accounts, Business Economic Notes, Computation of profits, Assessment of profits, Capital allowances, Losses, The Enterprise Allowance, National Insurance, Special situations	
7	**Personal Pensions**	59
	Eligible individuals, Benefits on retirement, Tax relief on premiums, Retirement annuities, Waiver of Premium benefits, Personal pension planning	
8	**Investment Income**	65
	Tax-free income, Rental income, Rent a room, Dividends and interest, Accrued income, Single premium bonds, Tax-Exempt Special Savings Accounts, Personal Equity Plans, Friendly Societies, Business Expansion Scheme, Enterprise Investment Scheme, Joint income	
9	**The Family Unit**	75
	Marriage, Children, Separation and divorce, Old age, Death	

10	The Overseas Element	81

Domicile, Residence and Ordinary Residence, Working abroad — long absences, Working abroad — shorter absences, Leaving the UK permanently, Allowances for non-UK residents, Double taxation relief, Taking up UK residence

11	Capital Gains Tax	86

Rate of tax, Husband and wife, Losses, The computation of gains, The indexation allowance, Assets owned on 31 March 1982, Quoted stocks and shares, Unquoted investments, Assets held on 6 April 1965, Your private residence, A second home, Chattels, Wasting assets, Part disposals, Business assets, Re-investment relief, Gifts, Deferred gains on business assets and gifts, Inheritances

12	Completing the Return	102

Income, Outgoings, Capital Gains, Allowances, Penalties

13	Assessments and Repayment Claims	114

Appeals, Repayment claims, Repayment supplement, Remission of tax, Normal dates for tax payments, Interest on overdue tax

14	Elections and Claims — Time Limits	118

15	Inheritance Tax	121

Potentially exempt transfers, Gifts with reservation, Lifetime gifts, Exemptions, Miscellaneous aspects, Rates of tax, Intestacy

16	Tax-Saving Hints	126

Personal allowances and reliefs, Interest payments and other outgoings, Earnings from employment, The self-employed, Personal pensions and other investments, Capital Gains Tax, Inheritance Tax

17	Looking Ahead: Self-assessment and Simplification of Personal Tax	132

Self-assessment (Tax returns, Procedures to protect revenue, Payment of tax, Records), Current Year basis of assessment (Introduction, Transitional arrangements, Losses, Capital allowances, Partnerships, Non-business income)

Tables 139

1. Inland Revenue explanatory booklets
2. Flat rate allowances for special clothing and the upkeep of tools — 1993/94
3. Rates of National Insurance Contributions for 1993/94
4. VAT notices and leaflets
5. Capital Gains Tax — The Indexation Allowance
6. Social Security Benefits

1993 Budget Measures 151

INTRODUCTION

1993 will go down in history as the year of two Budgets. The March Budget Statement was delivered by the former Chancellor, Mr. Lamont. His successor, Mr. Clarke, was responsible for last November's Budget. From now on only one Budget Statement will be made to Parliament each year – in the Autumn. It will deal with the Government's tax plans for the following tax year and spending targets for the next three years.

This revised edition of the Guide is intended primarily to set out the tax system from 6 April 1993 to 5 April 1994. It incorporates both the changes in legislation brought about by the 1993 Finance Act as well as those measures announced by Mr. Clarke to take effect during the tax year to 5 April 1994. The major proposals on taxation announced by the two Chancellors in their respective Budgets, which do not come into operation until after 5 April 1994, are detailed in the Supplement at the end of the book.

From 6 April 1994, the total tax burden on us all is set to increase. Personal allowances have been frozen. Mortgage interest tax relief is restricted to the 20% rate of tax. The married couple's and some other allowances will only attract tax relief at the fixed rate of 20%. Previously taxpayers benefited from these allowances at their top rate of tax. On top of these changes come increases in National Insurance Contributions and the introduction of VAT on fuel.

The Guide has been written to assist you in understanding the workings of our tax system and to enable you to look after your tax affairs with the minimum of difficulty. I hope the various elections and tax-saving hints I have mentioned offer some ways of helping you reduce your annual tax bill.

1

HOW THE TAX SYSTEM WORKS

Before we look at the different types of taxable income and the various allowances and reliefs you can claim, I thought it would be helpful to give you an outline of the functions of the Inland Revenue departments which operate our tax system. Overall authority for administering the legislation enacted by Government is vested in the Board of Inland Revenue. Although there are now many specialist departments within the Inland Revenue it is likely that your only direct contact with the Revenue will be through your Inspector and Collector of Taxes.

There are many tax offices spread out all over the country. Each tax office is headed up by a district inspector who has a support staff of inspectors and clerks.

The Inspector of Taxes
It is your Inspector of Taxes who sends out a Tax Return for you to complete every year. If you are either employed or a pensioner you can expect to receive this Return from the Inspector of Taxes who deals with the Pay-As-You-Earn affairs of your employer or his pension fund. It is not unusual for an employee's tax office to be many miles away from his home. For example, if you work in London your Inspector of Taxes is probably somewhere in Lancashire, Yorkshire, the West Country or Scotland. Where you are self-employed you will find that your local tax office handles your Tax Returns.

Not only is your Inspector of Taxes responsible for sending you a Tax Return to complete but you can also expect to receive notices of coding, assessments and general correspondence on your affairs from the same office. A notice of coding tells you what allowances and reliefs are due to you, so indicating that part of your salary which is tax free (see Chapter 4). An assessment is a calculation of the tax payable on a particular sort of income after deduction of any allowances or reliefs which are due to you.

2 HOW THE TAX SYSTEM WORKS

The Collector of Taxes

The only responsibility of the Collector of Taxes, as the name implies, is to collect the tax which is due from you. Whenever your Inspector of Taxes sends an assessment to you the Collector is notified of the tax payable. If it is not paid by the due date you can expect to receive further demands until payment is made. Should you still fail to make payment the Collector will eventually institute proceedings for recovery of the tax by distraint.

If you are late in paying your tax and incur an interest charge it is the Collector who sends you a demand for the interest.

You can provide for the payment of a future tax liability by purchasing a Certificate of Tax Deposit. Certificates can be bought from the Collector of Taxes. They earn interest from the date of purchase up until the normal due date for payment of the liability (see Chapter 13). The interest is taxable.

Communicating with the Inland Revenue

On any straightforward matter where it helps you to have a quick answer it is better to telephone your tax office. Unless you specifically ask to speak to the Inspector you will be put through to one of his assistants who will usually be able to answer your enquiry. On a more involved aspect of your tax affairs I suggest you write to the tax office. Always remember to quote your reference number in any correspondence. Unfortunately, you may sometimes have difficulty in understanding the reply to your letter. I hope that by the time you have read this book you will be in a better position to decipher any correspondence, which at first sight looks horribly complicated. There are, of course, occasions when an exchange of letters will be initiated by your tax office. Where this happens, try to reply promptly and give the information requested in a clear and concise manner.

There may be times when a particular matter concerning your tax affairs can best be resolved by a detailed discussion. Then is the time to arrange a visit to your tax office. Where this is situated a long way from your place of employment or home you can always arrange to go to the nearest PAYE Enquiry Office. Remember that the Inspector of Taxes and his assistants are not responsible for making the legislation in our tax system. If you think you are being unfairly treated by the law there is no point in adopting an aggressive attitude at the interview. You will usually get a helpful response, especially if you adopt a polite approach to the Inspector or his assistant.

Where the Inspector has reason to believe that there has either been an omission of income from your Returns or an under-declaration of business profits, he will often request a formal interview. At such a meeting the Inspector can be expected to pursue a wide-ranging line of questioning about your business activities and spending habits. You may well find some of the questions unreasonable or objectionable but it is one of the Inspector's duties to detect tax evasion and collect the tax due on the undeclared income. In the circumstances, the Inspector's line of questioning will probably be justified.

The Taxpayer's Charter
The Taxpayer's Charter sets out the principles which the Inland Revenue aim to meet in handling taxpayers' affairs. It emphasizes the Inland Revenue's commitment to providing high quality customer service and highlights the help taxpayers can expect to receive, and the ways in which they can complain if they are not satisfied. Under the Charter, taxpayers can expect the Inland Revenue to be fair, helpful, efficient and accountable. The text of the Charter is as follows:

You are entitled to expect the Inland Revenue
To be fair

By settling your tax affairs impartially
By expecting you to pay only what is due under the law
By treating everyone with equal fairness

To help you

To get your tax affairs right
To understand your rights and obligations
By providing clear leaflets and forms
By giving you information and assistance
at our enquiry offices
By being courteous at all times

To provide an efficient service

By settling your tax affairs promptly and accurately
By keeping your private affairs strictly confidential
By using the information you give us only as allowed by the law
By keeping to a minimum your costs of
complying with the the law
By keeping our costs down

To be accountable for what we do

By setting standards for ourselves and publishing how
well we live up to them

If you are not satisfied

We will tell you exactly how to complain
You can ask for your tax affairs to be looked at again
You can appeal to an independent tribunal
Your MP can refer your complaint to the Ombudsman

In return, we need you

To be honest
To give us accurate information
To pay your tax on time

The Taxpayer's Charter provides the foundation for a number of customer service initiatives. These include:

- redesigning some of the most commonly used forms to make them easier to understand;

- publishing a new series of leaflets which will tell particular groups of people (such as small-business people, pensioners and school leavers) what kind of help and level of services each can expect;

- trying out more flexible hours for Tax Enquiry Centres in order to test public demand;

- seeking people's views about the service they receive;

- publishing a leaflet explaining how people who are dissatisfied can complain;

- appointing Customer Service Managers with specific responsibility for customer service;

- setting and publishing standards for replying to taxpayers' letters. This includes setting turnaround times for dealing with post;
- asking staff who deal directly with the public to wear name badges and be ready to give their name on the telephone and in letters (except in cases where there is a real threat to the safety of the member of staff).

Complaints

Most complaints about the Inland Revenue's handling of people's tax affairs are satisfactorily settled by the local tax office concerned. Where taxpayers are not satisfied with the response from the local office, they can complain to senior local management or, if they wish, to the Inland Revenue's head office, to a member of Parliament, or to the Parliamentary Commissioner for Administration.

Now taxpayers, who are not satisfied with the Inland Revenue's response to their complaints, will have the option of putting their case to the new Inland Revenue Adjudicator. Complaints will normally go to the Adjudicator only when they have been considered by senior local management and if the taxpayer is still not satisfied with the response he or she has received. The Adjudicator will review all the facts and aim to reach a decision as speedily as possible. Unless there are very exceptional circumstances the Inland Revenue will normally accept the Adjudicator's decision.

The Adjudicator will consider complaints about the way in which the Inland Revenue has handled someone's tax affairs – for example, complaints about excessive delay, errors, discourtesy – or the way in which the Inland Revenue has exercised discretion. The Board of Inland Revenue will receive an annual report from the Adjudicator. It hopes this will be a useful mechanism for identifying areas where problems are occurring and where changes may need to be considered.

Changes in legislation

Every year, the Chancellor of the Exchequer makes his annual Budget Statement. Not only does the Chancellor choose the occasion to introduce new or amending legislation to our tax laws, but he also announces the rates of tax and allowances for the following year.

The changes in legislation necessary to implement the Chancellor's proposals are subsequently published in a Finance Bill. The clauses in the Bill are debated and amendments are often proposed to some of them. Subsequently, the Bill is passed by both Houses of Parliament and receives the Royal Assent. It is then republished as a Finance Act.

It is the fiscal legislation passed by Parliament which is administered by the Inland Revenue. On occasions when the law is either unclear or ambiguous the Inland Revenue publish a Statement of Practice showing how they intend to interpret it. There are also times when the Inland Revenue do not seek to apply the strict letter of the law. These are published as a list of Extra-Statutory Concessions.

The Inland Revenue also publish a number of booklets on different aspects of our tax system. A list of the most helpful booklets is set out in Table 1 at the end of the book.

Income Tax rates for 1993/94

Under our tax system, the tax (or fiscal) year runs from each 6 April to the following 5 April.

The rates of tax applying to taxable income for 1993/94 are:

Band of Taxable Income	Rate of Tax	Tax on Band	Cumulative Tax
£	%	£	£
0 – 2,500	20	500	500
2,501 – 23,700	25	5,300	5,800
over 23,700	40		

The rate of 20% is known as the lower rate. The basic rate is 25% and tax at 40% is referred to as the higher rate.

Beginning with 1993/94, dividends from your UK shareholdings form the top part of your taxable income. The tax at the basic rate on this income is restricted to 20%.

The law provides that the band of income taxable at the basic rate is to be increased each tax year in line with the movement in the Retail Prices Index during the year to the end of September prior to the tax year. As with the main personal allowances the Treasury can, however, order an increase different to the statutory commitment, providing Parliament agrees.

2

PERSONAL ALLOWANCES AND RELIEFS

The rates of the various personal allowances for 1993/94 are:

		£
Personal		3,445
Married couple's		1,720
Additional personal		1,720
Widow's bereavement		1,720
Age		
— personal	(age 65–74)	4,200
— married couple's	(age 65–74)	2,465
— personal	(age 75 and over)	4,370
— married couple's	(age 75 and over)	2,505
Relief for blind person		1,080

There is a section in your Tax Return for you to claim the particular allowances to which you are entitled. They are deducted from your total income in calculating the amount on which you pay Income Tax each year.

The rates of allowances tend to vary from year to year. This is because the law provides that the allowances in the table above, with the exception of the relief for a blind person, are to go up at the beginning of each tax year. This upwards movement is in line with the increase in the Retail Prices Index during the year to the end of September prior to the tax year. The Treasury can, however, order an increase different from the statutory commitment providing Parliament agrees.

For 1993/94 all the personal and age-related allowances remain unchanged.

Personal allowance

Every man and woman, single or married, is entitled to the personal allowance. This can be of particular benefit to a married woman. She is able to set her personal allowance against a salary or business profits, investment income, or occupational and/or State Pension(s) including one paid to her based on her husband's contributions.

Married couple's allowance

A married man whose wife is living with him can claim the married couple's allowance. In the year of marriage the amount of the married couple's allowance depends upon the time during the year that the marriage took place. The allowance is reduced by one-twelfth for every complete month from 6 April up to the date of the wedding.

Illustration
A husband who was married on 18 August 1993 receives an allowance of £1,147 for 1993/94 calculated as follows:

	£
Married couple's allowance	1,720
Less: Reduction	
$4/12 \times £1,720$	573
1993/94 Allowance	1,147

The married couple's allowance is not reduced in the year when couples separate or in the year of death of either spouse.

A wife can elect to receive one-half of the married couple's allowance. She does not need her husband's consent to make this election. Alternatively, the allowance can be deducted wholly from the wife's total income, instead of the husband's income. This sort of election must be made jointly by husband and wife. However, the husband can subsequently, on his own, elect to take back one-half of the allowance.

All the above elections refer only to the standard married couple's allowance of £1,720 and not to the age-related allowances. An election must be made on the special Inland Revenue form 18 which is reproduced here. Any of the three elections must normally be made before the beginning of the tax year for which it is to have effect. It will then apply for that year and each succeeding tax year until altered by subsequent election or notice of withdrawal. A withdrawal is not effective until the tax year after that in which it is given to the Inland Revenue.

MARRIED COUPLE'S ALLOWANCE 9

Inland Revenue

/

Please use both lines of this reference if you write or call. It will help to avoid delay.

Transferring the married couple's allowance

The married couple's allowance is given to the husband to set against his income unless you ask for a different arrangement. This request is called an election. You should use this form to tell me if you want to change the existing allocation of the allowance.

1. A married couple may jointly decide that they want the married couple's allowance to be given to the wife. The husband will then get none of the allowance. (But see note 1 if either of you is aged 65 or over.)

2. They may later jointly agree to change that decision so that the allowance is given to the husband instead of to the wife. The wife will then get none of the allowance.

3. If a husband is receiving all the married couple's allowance, his wife may ask for one half of the amount of the allowance to be given to her instead. The husband's agreement is not necessary.

4. If a wife is receiving all the married couple's allowance, her husband may ask for one half of the amount of the allowance to be given to him instead. The wife's agreement is not necessary.

You must tell me your decision by completing this form. You should return it to me before the start (on 6 April) of the tax year in which it is to operate. Before you begin please read the notes attached.

If you wish to do either 1. or 2. above, please complete Section A over the page. You and your husband or wife must both sign and date it.

If you wish to do either 3. or 4. above, please complete Section B over the page and sign and date it.

Please return the form to me intact. Do not complete the acknowledgement on the back page. I will use this to confirm that I have accepted your request to change the allocation of the married couple's allowance.

H M Inspector of Taxes

District date stamp

10 PERSONAL ALLOWANCES AND RELIEFS

*Complete **either** Section A **or** Section B, in CAPITAL letters*

Section A

We jointly agree that the married couple's allowance* be given to _____

insert name

This is to operate from 6 April 19

	Husband	Wife
Names in full, surname first		
Tax references *if known*	/	/
National Insurance numbers *if known*		
Private address(es) *including postcode*		
Signatures and dates		

Section B

I elect that one half of the married couple's allowance* which my husband/wife _____

insert his or her name

is now claiming be given to me.

This election is to operate from 6 April 19

Your names in full, surname first

Your tax reference *if known*

Your National Insurance number *if known*

Private address *including postcode*

Signature and date

Full names of your husband or wife, surname first

Their tax reference *if known*

Their National Insurance number *if known*

* if either of you is aged 65 or over the transfer is limited to an amount equal to all or half the married couple's allowance for those under 65

There are two exceptions to the time limit for making the elections. The first of these applies to the year of marriage where a notice can immediately be given in respect of the reduced married couple's allowance for that year. The second exception applies for the first tax year for which an election is made. Here an election may be made within the first 30 days of that tax year so long as the Inspector of Taxes was advised in writing before the start of the tax year of an intention to make the election.

If none of these elections is made, the husband is entitled to the full married couple's allowance. Where he has a sufficiently low taxable income and cannot make full use of his married couple's allowance he can transfer any excess allowance to his wife. Alternatively, if, following an election, a wife does not have sufficient taxable income against which to set off her married couple's allowance she can transfer the excess to her husband. In both these cases the notice to transfer the excess allowance to the other spouse must be given within six years after the end of the tax year.

Age allowances

A pensioner whose income is below a specified annual limit is entitled to higher allowances: these are known as the personal age and married couple's age allowances. To be eligible the elderly taxpayer must be over the age of 65 during part or all of the tax year. There are higher age allowances for a pensioner over 75 for part or all of the tax year. The amount of the personal age allowance depends entirely on the age of the elderly taxpayer. So long as one spouse is at least 65 years old the husband will be due the married couple's age allowance. The level of this allowance depends on the age of the elder spouse.

Illustration

A couple who were 65 years old (husband) and 62 years old (wife) during the 1993/94 tax year are entitled to allowances of £6,665 and £3,445 as follows:

	Husband £	Wife £
Personal age	4,200	3,445
Married couple's age	2,465	–
Total allowances	£6,665	£3,445

Another couple had their 73rd birthday (husband) and 77th birthday (wife) in 1993/94. Their total allowances are £6,705 and £4,370 as follows:

	Husband £	Wife £
Personal age	4,200	4,370
Married couple's age	2,505	–
Total allowances	£6,705	£4,370

As the age allowances are designed to help those pensioners who are less well off, they reduce where their income before tax rises above £14,200 for 1993/94. This reduction in age allowances is one-half of the amount by which total income exceeds the stated limit of £14,200, although it cannot take the rate of the allowance below the level of either the single or married couple's allowances as the case may be. Whether an elderly spouse can claim the personal age allowance depends solely on the amount of his or her income. However, any restriction of the married couple's age allowance is measured solely by the husband's income. Any part of the husband's married couple's age allowance that is unused because, for example, he has a low income, can be transferred over to his wife in the same way that any unused part of the ordinary married couple's allowance can be transferred.

Illustration

An elderly couple, aged 79 (husband) and 69 (wife), whose income amounted to £7,500 and £14,800 respectively during 1993/94 are entitled to allowances of £6,875 and £3,900 as follows:

	Husband £	Wife £
Income before tax		
State pensions	2,917	1,752
Pensions from former employers	1,783	6,548
Investment income	2,800	6,500
	£7,500	£14,800

Allowances

Personal age	4,370	4,200
Married couple's age	2,505	–
	£6,875	£4,200
Less: Reduction		
½ × 600 (£14,800 – £14,200)	–	300
1993/94 Allowances	£6,875	£3,900

It follows that no measure of personal age allowance is due to an elderly taxpayer (aged 65–74) whose income exceeds £15,710 for 1993/94. For a pensioner aged 75 or over the maximum income limit is increased to £16,050.

The upper income limits for a husband beyond which no measure of married couple's age allowance is due for 1993/94 are:

	Age of Elderly Spouse	
Husband's Age	65–74	Over 74
	£	£
Under 65	15,690	Variable
65–74	17,200	17,280
Over 74	–	17,620

The income limit for age allowances goes up each tax year in the same way as the main personal allowances.

Arising out of the transition to Independent Taxation a special personal allowance may be claimed in certain circumstances by a husband under 65 whose wife was over 74 on 5 April 1990. This special personal allowance amounts to £3,540 for 1993/94.

Additional personal allowance

To qualify for this allowance you must be a person such as a widow, widower or divorcee, who is not entitled to claim the married couple's allowance, or a married man whose wife is either physically incapacitated or mentally infirm. In either event you must have at least one child living with you who fulfils certain conditions. If the child is your own he or she must be under 16 at the start of the tax year. If older, he or she must still be at school or attending a full-time course at a university, college or similar place of education, or undergoing a training course for at least two years with an employer in some trade or profession. Where the child living with you is not your own then he or she must be under 18 years old at the beginning of the tax year and looked after at your own expense.

No matter how many children you may have living with you who fulfil these tests only one allowance can be claimed. If more than one person is in a position to claim the allowance for the same child then it will be apportioned between them.

A man and a woman who are not married to each other but live together as man and wife are only entitled to the additional personal allowance for the youngest child living with them.

Only for the tax year in which a man, who is entitled to the additional personal allowance, marries can he choose whether to claim that allowance instead of the married couple's allowance. He will probably do so because this, unlike the married couple's allowance, is not reduced in the year of marriage. A husband with a low income will probably want to be given the reduced married couple's allowance because he can elect to transfer any unused part of this allowance to his wife, which he cannot do with the additional personal allowance.

In the year of separation there has always been the possibility, however remote, that someone could claim both the married couple's allowance and additional personal allowance. Now that the married couple's allowance is more freely transferable between husband and wife, special rules, for the year of separation only, have been introduced to limit the total allowance available. This is achieved by restricting the normal additional personal allowance where the claimant also receives the married couple's allowance.

Widow's bereavement allowance

Providing her husband was entitled to the married couple's allowance at the time of his death, a widow can claim this allowance for both the tax year in which her husband dies and the following tax year as long as she has not remarried by the beginning of that year.

In the year of her husband's death a widow can set all the allowances due to her against her total income for that tax year. For that year she cannot obtain both the bereavement allowance and a transferred married couple's allowance. However, if her husband's income was such that he could not use the full married couple's or married couple's age allowance then the balance will automatically be given to his widow.

Blind person's relief

This relief is given to a registered blind person. If both husband and wife are blind they may each claim the relief. If a husband or wife is unable to use up his or her blind person's relief fully because of insufficient income, any unused part of the relief can be transferred to the other spouse even if he or she is not blind.

Transfer of allowances

There are special rules to cater for a married couple who found that their total allowances were reduced when Independent Taxation was introduced. They apply to a couple who were married and living together in both 1989/90 and 1990/91 provided they did not elect for the wife's earnings to be separately taxed in 1989/90. Where the husband had a low income in 1990/91 and was unable to benefit from his full personal allowance he could elect to transfer his surplus personal allowance to his wife. He can also do so again in later years whenever he has an income which is insufficient to utilize his full personal allowance. However, where a husband's income for 1990/91 was such that he could benefit from his full personal allowance in that year he will never be able to transfer any part of his personal allowance to his wife.

Illustration

A young married couple are substantially dependent on the wife's salary. During 1993/94 she earned £14,000. Her husband's salary was only £1,600. The married couple's and personal allowances which can be transferred to the wife total £2,115 as follows:

Married couple's allowance

	£	£
Married couple's allowance		1,720
Husband's salary	1,600	
Less: Personal allowance	3,445	
		—
		£1,720

Personal allowances

	£	£
Husband's total allowances for 1989/90		7,160
Less: Husband's total income for 1993/94	1,600	
Wife's total allowances for 1993/94 (including the transferred married couple's allowance)	5,165	
		6,765
		£395

These rules should not be confused with those which deal with the married couple's, married couple's age or blind person's allowances. These can be transferred in any tax year.

Relief on life assurance premiums

These days life assurance serves many purposes. They range from providing for the payment of lump sums on death, either to pay off the amount of an outstanding mortgage or to leave a lump sum for the deceased's dependants, to other uses which can often serve as tax-efficient forms of investment.

The amount of tax relief on life assurance premiums is at the fixed rate of 12.5% on policies taken out before 14 March 1984. It should not be necessary for you to claim this since the premiums paid to the life assurance company are after deduction of the 12.5% tax relief. There are occasions when some or all of this relief can be withdrawn, and then a payment to the Inland Revenue will have to be made for the tax relief which has been lost. For example, the amount of such premiums which can be paid in any tax year without restriction of the tax relief is limited to £1,500 or one sixth of your total income before allowances, whichever is greater.

Illustration

A taxpayer pays annual life assurance premiums of £1,700 before tax relief. If his income is:

(a) £12,000, the 12.5% tax relief is unrestricted;
(b) £8,000, he will only receive the 12.5% tax relief on premiums of £1,500.

Premiums payable on a life assurance policy taken out after 13 March 1984 do not attract any tax relief. The same applies to future premiums payable on a policy taken out before that date if, after 13 March 1984, the benefits secured under the policy are varied or its terms extended.

3

INTEREST PAYMENTS AND OTHER OUTGOINGS

As the opportunities to claim tax relief for interest paid on borrowed money are limited, you should be aware of the few occasions when you can do so. It is important to appreciate that the purpose for which a loan is raised governs whether the interest on it will be eligible for tax relief. How the loan is secured is irrelevant.

Generally the interest on which tax relief is due is deducted from your total income in the year of payment. This general rule does not apply where you borrow money to buy a property which you let out: this is dealt with later on in the chapter.

Your own home
If you have borrowed money from a building society, a bank or some other source to help you buy your home you will receive tax relief on the interest you pay each year. Your home can be a house or a flat; it may even be a houseboat or a caravan.

It is not only the purchase price of your home which governs the maximum amount of the loan on which interest qualifies for tax relief. The incidental costs of buying your home such as surveyor's and solicitor's fees and stamp duty all count as part of the cost price of your home.

Interest relief is no longer given on new or replacement home improvement loans. However, interest on a home improvement loan, for example the installation of double glazing, taken out before 6 April 1988 still qualifies for tax relief.

There is an overall loan limit for mortgage interest tax relief: for 1993/94 this is £30,000. It applies to any one home rather than to each borrower. Unmarried couples jointly buying a home have to share the maximum limit between them.

Where two or more unmarried individuals share a home and each takes out a loan or has a share in a joint loan to purchase their home, the £30,000 limit is allocated between or amongst them in equal shares. For example, three individuals living together are each entitled to a limit of £10,000. Each individual qualifies for tax relief on the interest he or she pays on his or her loan or share of a joint loan up to £10,000. There are special rules to deal with unequal loans where the borrowers between them are not able to use up the full £30,000 limit, even though their total mortgages come to more than the limit. For example:

>A has a loan of £21,000
>B has a loan of £9,000
>C has a loan of £5,000

Without a transfer of allowances the result would be:

>A gets tax relief on £10,000 with £11,000 unrelieved
>B gets tax relief on £9,000
>C gets tax relief on £5,000
>Total relief on   £24,000

In this example, B and C can transfer relief on £1,000 and £5,000 respectively to A, increasing his entitlement to relief on interest on £16,000. As a result, interest on £30,000 of the total loans of £35,000 qualifies for tax relief.

Mortgages taken out before the beginning of August 1988 are unaffected by these rules. In these cases the limit of £30,000 applies to each borrower.

Married couples can share their mortgage interest tax relief in any way they want by completing an allocation of interest election. A couple may benefit from making this election if only one of them is (a) liable to tax and the loan is not within the MIRAS scheme or (b) over 65 with an income above the limit for age allowance.

An election for the 1993/94 tax year can be made at any time up to 5 April 1995 or within such longer period as the Board of Inland Revenue may in any particular case allow. It will then also apply for 1994/95 unless the couple jointly elect on or before 5 April 1996 to withdraw it. In its first year of operation an election cannot be retracted once it has been made.

If you are employed in some capacity that requires you to live in accommodation provided by your employer you can still in certain specific circumstances obtain mortgage interest relief on a loan to buy your own home. This also applies if you are self-employed and the terms of your trade or profession are such that you must live in accommodation provided for your use.

Most people move home at some time during their lifetime. It is often impossible to arrange for the sale of your present home to coincide with the purchase of your new one. To overcome such difficulties, borrowers moving home, who are unable to sell their existing homes, can continue to claim mortgage interest relief in respect of their old home. They are allowed this relief for a period of up to one year (or longer, at the Inland Revenue's discretion) after moving out. Nor do they have to take out a mortgage on their new home.

Many borrowers are now faced with mortgages which exceed the value of their homes. If they want to move they cannot pay off all the outstanding mortgage out of the sale proceeds of their home. It is now easier for borrowers with negative equity in their homes to move on. Lenders can keep the old loan in existence, rather than having to redeem it and advancing a new one, without the borrower losing entitlement to mortgage interest relief. The amount of the deemed new mortgage on which interest ranks for tax relief, subject to the overall limitation of £30,000, is the lower of the outstanding mortgage and the purchase price of the new home.

Most of you are making your regular mortgage repayments after deduction of tax at the basic rate on the interest element in each repayment. This procedure is known as 'Mortgage Interest Relief at Source' – MIRAS for short. You do not have to pay this tax over to the Inland Revenue. This applies even where you have no taxable income, or where your income is less than your personal allowances. If your mortgage exceeds the limitation of £30,000 on which interest qualifies for tax relief you will receive relief on that part of the total interest payable equivalent to this limit. This relief is obtained either through the tax deduction scheme or your PAYE coding. Only tax at the basic rate is taken off the interest at the time of payment. The interest is disregarded in working out your tax liability at the top rate of 40%.

A home for a dependent relative
It is no longer possible to get tax relief on a mortgage, within the overall £30,000 limit, taken out to buy a home for a

dependent relative. This change applied to new and replacement loans taken out on or after 6 April 1988. Tax relief is preserved on existing qualifying loans.

The relative must be either a pensioner or too unwell to look after himself or herself. Where the relative is the claimant's mother or mother-in-law, it is sufficient if she is widowed, separated or divorced.

Let property

Interest on a loan taken out to buy or improve a property which you rent out is tax deductable. The interest is set against the rental income from the property. Should the interest payable in a tax year exceed the rents receivable in the same year, the excess can only be carried forward to future years.

Illustration

A property was bought in 1988 with the assistance of a £60,000 loan. It is let and the rents less expenses came to £7,000 and £12,000 during 1992/93 and 1993/94 respectively.

	1992/93		1993/94
	£		£
Rents less expenses	7,000		12,000
Less: Loan interest paid	9,000	6,600	
Deficit carried forward	£2,000	2,000	8,600
1993/94 Taxable Income			£3,400

The property must be let at a commercial rent for at least 26 weeks in any period of 52 weeks. When it is not let it must either be available for letting or be undergoing repairs or renovations.

Business loans

Most businesses need to borrow money at some time for one purpose or another. Interest on any such borrowings is allowable as a deduction against your business profits providing the borrowed money is used for business purposes. It does not matter for this purpose whether the borrowings arise because your bank account goes overdrawn, or because you take out a loan for some specific purpose connected with your business.

If you need to borrow to buy an asset – such as a car or a piece of machinery – for use in your business, the interest you pay will qualify for tax relief but will be restricted where the asset is also used privately.

If you are about to become a member of a partnership, you may need to borrow money to purchase a share in the partnership or to contribute capital for use in its business. If that is the case, the interest on the borrowings will qualify for tax relief.

Alternatively, you may have business connections with a private company. The interest on a loan raised so you can either acquire shares in the company or lend it money for use in its business will qualify for tax relief. You must either own at least 5% of the company's share capital or have at least some shareholding and work for the greater part of your time in the business.

Employees who need to borrow to buy shares in their company as part of an employee buy-out are allowed tax relief on the interest.

Charitable deeds of covenant

Deeds of covenant are an effective way of making a donation to a charity. To be valid for tax purposes, a deed must be capable of providing for regular annual payments over a minimum period of more than three years. The payer must deduct Income Tax at the basic rate from every payment under a deed. The tax deducted can be retained providing the payer has suffered tax at the basic rate which is at least equivalent to the tax deducted from all covenanted payments during a tax year.

As an incentive to individuals with high incomes, they are allowed to deduct covenanted payments to charities from their income in calculating their tax liabilities at the higher rate of 40%.

Under Independent Taxation tax relief on charitable deeds of covenant is only allowed against the payer's income. If the payer is not liable to Income Tax on his or her income alone, payments under a charitable deed of covenant may no longer qualify for tax relief by the payer. One way of overcoming this situation is to switch the covenant to the tax-paying spouse. It is also conceivable that some couples will find they can no longer benefit from higher rate tax relief on their charitable covenants or alternatively that the amount of tax relief is restricted.

Quite often individuals making covenants do not draw them up in a form which is legally effective. To help charities and individual donors ensure that their covenants are legally effective guidance notes are available from the Inland Revenue. They suggest model forms of words which charities and individuals may use if they so wish and deal with a number of other practical points about the conditions which covenants must satisfy to be eligible for tax relief.

Gift Aid

Gift Aid is an Income Tax relief for single cash gifts by individuals to charities. Each gift must be at least £250, net of basic rate tax. There is no maximum annual limit for gifts by any one donor. As with regular donations to charities under Deed of covenant, payments under the Gift Aid Scheme are made net of tax at the basic rate. You must give the charity a certificate – Form R190 (SD) – for each separate payment so it can claim the tax back from the Inland Revenue. Individuals with high incomes can deduct their gifts from their income in calculating how much tax they must pay at the top 40% tax rate.

Gifts in kind are not allowed – only cash gifts. Gifts will not qualify for the relief if they are linked with any purchase of property by the charity from the donor or where they are in return for services or benefits.

Payroll deduction scheme

If you are in employment there may be a further alternative way open for you to make donations to charity. If your employer operates such a scheme through an Approved Agency Charity, your charitable donations can be made through your employer by way of regular deductions from your salary. Employers are not bound to launch such schemes and employees can choose whether to participate in them. If you do so, you will be entitled to tax relief on donations not exceeding £900 annually.

Private medical insurance

Tax relief is allowed on premiums paid for private medical insurance where the premiums are paid under an eligible contract and the cover is provided for individuals aged 60 and over.

For joint contracts covering a husband and wife then only one of them needs to be over 60. Relief is available to the individual actually paying the premium whether it be for himself, a relative or friend. The contracts should provide cover for medical or surgical treatment in the UK carried out by a qualified practitioner. Your insurers should be able to advise you whether or not your contract is eligible for tax relief and, if not, what alterations are required so that it can qualify.

Tax relief at the basic rate is obtained by deducting Income Tax at 25% from the premiums paid to the insurance company. To claim relief at the higher rate of 40%, if due, a certificate should be obtained from the insurance company certifying the premium paid. In turn, this should be submitted to the Inspector of Taxes dealing with your tax affairs.

Vocational training

You can get tax relief on payments you make for your own vocational training. The training costs which qualify for this new tax relief must lead to a National Vocational Qualification, or the Scottish equivalent, up to and including level 4. From 1 January 1994 the relief is extended to level 5. However, the relief does not extend to general education qualifications, such as GCSE's or 'A' levels, even where these are taken as a preliminary to Vocational Qualification Study. Nor, from 1 January 1994, is tax relief allowed to children under 16, and 16-18 year-olds in full-time schooling. The same applies for training undertaken wholly or mainly for recreational purposes or as a leisure activity.

The new relief is given on study, examination or assessment costs. Not included are the cost of books or equipment nor travelling and subsistence expenses.

There are two main conditions which have to be satisfied by the trainee. Firstly, you must be a UK resident. Secondly, you must not be getting, or eligible for, assistance under Government Schemes such as student grant awards or employment training.

You get the relief directly when paying your fees. All you have to do is deduct an amount equal to the basic rate of tax of 25% from the study, examination or assessment fees you pay. You can get this relief even if you are a non-taxpayer. Also, higher rate taxpayers will be allowed relief on their vocational training costs at the top rate of 40%.

4

EARNINGS FROM EMPLOYMENT

Most of you will be familiar with at least some part or other of the Pay As You Earn (PAYE) system. It provides a mechanism for collecting the tax due on the earnings of those people in employment. Employers must deduct Income Tax from the earnings of their employees and every month the total of these deductions has to be paid over to the Inland Revenue. The PAYE taken off an employee's earnings is treated as a credit against the overall amount of tax payable by the employee for the tax year in question. In working out the amount of tax to deduct from each employee's salary or pay packet, the employer takes into account each individual's own allowances and other reliefs. This is possible because the Inland Revenue issue employers with a code number for each employee. In turn the code number incorporates each employee's allowances and reliefs. The system allows for these to be spread evenly throughout the tax year to avoid any substantial variation in the amount of tax deducted from each salary cheque or pay packet.

The sort of earnings which count as taxable income from an employment are:

> An annual salary or wage
> Bonus
> Overtime
> Commission
> Tips or gratuities
> Holiday pay
> Sick pay
> Earnings from a part-time employment
> Directors' fees or other remuneration
> Benefits-in-kind

All directors and employees are taxed on the earnings they actually receive in a tax year.

Code numbers

I have already mentioned that each employee is issued with a code number by the tax office. In theory the code number should ensure that the correct amount of tax has been deducted from your earnings by the end of the tax year. The system can only work properly and effectively if your local tax office is kept informed of any changes in your personal circumstances which affect the amount of your allowances or reliefs. For example, most if not all notices of coding for the 1994 tax year commencing on 6 April 1994 were issued during the early part of the year. This was before taxpayers came to complete their 1994 Income Tax Returns. The Return requires a report of each person's income for the tax year just finished – the year to 5 April 1994 – but the claim for allowances is for the following year – the year to 5 April 1995. It follows that the information on which all the code numbers for 1994/95 have been based is that of the previous year. This is why it is important you should check your code number for 1994/95 and write to your tax office setting out any alterations that are required to your allowances or reliefs. If the rate of any allowance has been altered in the Budget there is no need for you to communicate with your tax office – your employer will automatically have been instructed by the Inland Revenue about how to deal with this.

On the following page is an illustration of a notice of coding for 1994/95. It shows the taxpayer is a married man. His allowances for 1994/95 are £5,165 before deductions. The first three of these relate to benefits-in-kind in the form of a company car and private medical insurance cover provided by the taxpayer's employer. Some of the types of taxable expenses and benefits are dealt with later on in the chapter. The coding notice illustrates how the tax payable on benefits-in-kind is usually collected. This is done by restricting the taxpayer's allowances by the value of the benefits-in-kind. In the illustration they come to £3,850, reducing the allowances to £1,315.

Beginning with the 1994/95 tax year some of the allowances mentioned in Chapter 2 will only attract tax relief at the fixed rate of 20%. This applies for all taxpayers. The allowances subject to this restriction are the married couple's, the two age-related married couple's, the additional personal and the widow's bereavement. Also affected is the relief for maintenance payments mentioned in Chapter 9. The fourth

CODE NUMBERS

Inland Revenue

Notice of your income tax code

Your employer or pension payer will use your tax code to ensure you pay the right amount of tax under Pay As You Earn (PAYE)

From: H M Inspector of Taxes

Fieldgate District
Fieldgate House,
Fieldgate TA6 7DP

MR. D. JONES
79 ACORN STREET
FIELDGATE
TA6 2PY

You should quote both numbers below if you contact us.

195/F249

FX 57 30 29 C

Date
24.01.94

The net allowances figure below shows how much of your pay or occupational pension will not have tax deducted from it. This figure is made up of your total allowances less the total reductions shown below. This notice of tax code replaces any previous notice for the year.

If you think the code is wrong, or if your personal circumstances change, you should tell your Tax Office immediately. The 'See note' column refers to notes in *PAYE: Understanding Your Tax Code* (leaflet P3(T)).

See note	Allowances	£	See note	Less amounts taken away to cover items shown below	£
17	Personal Allowance	3445	25	Medical Insurance	360
17	Married Allowance	1720	25	Benefits (Car)	2680
			25	Benefits (Car Fuel)	810
			33	Allowance restriction	340
			29	Tax Unpaid £120	480

Less total reductions 4670

Total allowances 5165

Net allowances - the amount of your pay or occupational pension from which tax will not be deducted 495

Your tax code is worked out from your net allowances. Your code for the year to 5 April 1995 is 49T   See note A overleaf

P2(T)

deduction in the coding notice illustrates the procedure for collecting the right amount of tax from the married man on his married couple's allowance. By restricting the net allowance to an effective amount of £1,380 (£1,720−£340) he will receive tax relief of £345 (£1,380 @ 25%) assuming he is a basic rate taxpayer. This is equivalent to the fixed rate of 20% on the full allowance of £1,720. If he were a 40% taxpayer the allowance restriction would be increased to £860. The final deduction is for tax underpaid for 1992/93 of £120. For any one of a number of reasons the allowances given in the coding notice may subsequently turn out to differ from those actually due to the taxpayer. If, as a result, there is an underpayment of tax, this is often collected in a later year, again by restricting allowances in the coding. In our illustration a reduction in allowances for 1994/95 of £480 will result in the Inland Revenue collecting the underpayment of £120 (£480 @ 25%) from the taxpayer during the year.

The combined effect of these adjustments is to leave the taxpayer with allowances of only £495 to be set against his salary for 1994/95. His code number will be 49T. Clearly, there is a direct link between the taxpayer's allowances and his code number. The suffix letter is added to the coding so that whenever there is a change in the rates of allowances it can automatically be implemented by the employer or payer of a pension. The various letters which can be part of the coding and what they stand for are as follows:

L — Is for a code which includes the personal allowance.

H — Stands for a code with the personal allowance plus either the married couple's allowance or the additional personal allowance.

P — Is for a code with the personal allowance for those aged 65-74.

V — Indicates the pensioner is entitled to both the personal and married couple's allowances for ages 65-74.

T — Applies in most other cases, for example:
* You ask your tax office not to use the letters L, H, P or V.
* You are due a personal or married couple's allowance for age 75 and over.
* You are not entitled to the full higher age-related allowance because your total income exceeds £14,200.
* You have a deduction from your allowances in your code for an item such as a car benefit.

If your code ends with the letter T your employer or payer of pension must then wait for instructions from your tax office before making any changes to the coding.

There are also a number of other codes. When no allowances have been given to you, you will receive an OT coding. Tax will be deducted at the basic rate, then at the higher rate of 40%, depending on your income. A BR coding is an instruction to your employer to deduct tax at the basic rate. Where the coding starts with the letter D, tax will be deducted at the higher rate of 40%. A NT coding means that no tax will be deducted.

Some employees may find that they have been allocated a K code. A K code is given to employees whose taxable benefits exceed their personal allowances. The amount of the negative allowances is then added to the pay or pension on which tax is to be paid. This system of K codes is designed to make taxpayers pay all the tax due on their benefits evenly throughout the tax year under the PAYE system, instead of receiving a demand at the end of the tax year for the lump sum owing.

The assessment

Shortly after the end of each tax year every employer sends in to the Inland Revenue a Return summarizing the names of all employees, their earnings during the tax year, and the Income Tax deducted from them. At the same time the employer hands out a Form P60 to every employee. This is a certificate of the employee's earnings for the past tax year and the Income Tax deducted from them. For most employees this corresponds with the tax due on their earnings. It is not then necessary for the Inland Revenue to issue an assessment. You can, however, always ask for one.

If you do receive an assessment it will show the earnings from all your employments during the past tax year together with the amounts of tax deducted by your employers. If you were provided with any benefits-in-kind, such as the use of a company car, the value of these will be shown in the assessment as an addition to your salary or wages. This information is supplied to your tax office by your employer on a Form P11D. The types of benefit-in-kind which are taxable are dealt with later on in this chapter. In addition to detailing your earnings, the assessment will also show the allowances and reliefs you have been given. The final part is a calculation of the Income Tax due for the year. The tax deducted by your employer under PAYE is set against the liability to arrive at the overall position. An assessment which shows an overpayment is always a welcome sight. It will usually come to you with a cheque in repayment of the tax overpaid. Alternatively, the Inspector of Taxes might ask you to complete a formal claim to repayment before the Inland Revenue send you their cheque. If you have not paid enough tax you may be asked to send the Inland Revenue a cheque for the underpayment. Where it is not substantial the Inspector of Taxes will usually decide to collect it by restricting your allowances through an amendment to your notice of coding. We have already seen how this works. You should check the assessment as soon as possible after you receive it. If you want to dispute the income on which your tax has been calculated the Inland Revenue allow you only thirty days to write about this.

It is Inland Revenue practice to dispense with an assessment on your employment income where the underpaid tax is £100 or less or there is a small overpayment of £7 or less.

Changing your job

Whenever you change your job your employer will hand you Parts 2 & 3 of a Form P45. This details your name and address, the name and address of your employer, your tax district and reference number, your code number at the date of leaving, and your salary and tax deductions for the tax year up to the date that you leave. Your employer will send the first part of the P45 form to his tax district.

You must hand Parts 2 & 3 of the Form P45 to your new employer. He will enter your address and the date you start your new job before sending Part 3 of the form to his own tax office. The information on the form enables your new employer to make the right deductions for Income Tax and National Insurance from your new salary or wage.

If you do not have a P45 to hand to your new employer, you will find that the deductions from your salary for Income Tax are equivalent to those of a single person without any other allowances or reliefs. This is known as the 'emergency' basis. If this happens you should either ask for and complete a Tax Return or send in sufficient information to your new employer's tax office so that the correct code number can be sent to your employer. If you have just left school or are taking up employment for the first time you should complete either a Form P15 or a Form P46 as a way of making sure that the right deductions for Income Tax are made from your salary.

Expenses

The rules which allow you to claim tax relief on expenses relating to an employment are extremely restrictive. They seek to deny tax relief on almost all types of expenses which are not ultimately borne by the employer. This is because the employee has to show that any expenditure is incurred 'wholly, exclusively and necessarily' while performing the duties of the employment. If the employer has not been prepared to foot the bill for the expenditure involved, then the Inland Revenue infer it was incurred more as a matter of choice than of necessity. Nevertheless, some business expenses paid personally are deductible from your income. Details of these should be entered on your Tax Return. They include:

- Annual subscriptions to a professional body.

- Business use of your own car and telephone.

- Clothing and upkeep of tools – the Inland Revenue and the Trade Unions have agreed flat rate allowances for the upkeep of tools and special clothing for most classes of industry. The current rates are set out in Table 2. As an alternative you may claim a deduction for the actual expenses on these items.

Remember that the cost of travelling between your home and the office is not allowable for tax purposes.

Most expenses you incur in your job or employment are probably borne by your employer, who either reimburses you on an expense claim or pays for them direct. Tax free for everyone are:

- Luncheon vouchers up to 15p per day.

- Free or subsidized meals in a staff canteen, providing the facilities can be used by all staff.

- Sporting and recreational facilities.

- Staff parties, providing the annual cost to the employer is no more than £50 per head.

- Routine health checks or medical screening.

- Awards for long service of at least 20 years. The cost of the articles purchased by the employer must not exceed £20 for each year of service.

Out-placement counselling costs.

Child-care facilities provided by an employer at the work place or elsewhere (but not on domestic premises).

Car-parking facilities at or near your place of work.

The cost of infrequent private transport when you have been working late and either public transport is no longer available or it would be unreasonable to expect you to use it at a late hour. Infrequent late working means a requirement to work until at least 9.00 p.m. not more than 60 times in a tax year.

Mileage allowances paid by an employer where employees use their car on business providing the mileage rate does no more than reimburse employees for the costs they have incurred on business travel. The tax-free rates laid down by the Inland Revenue 1993/94 are:-

	Business Use	
Engine Size	First 4,000 miles	Excess
Up to 1000 cc	26p	15p
1001 cc to 1500 cc	32p	18p
1501 cc to 2000 cc	40p	22p
Over 2000 cc	54p	30p

If an employer chooses to pay a uniform rate this should be the average of the middle two rates i.e. 36p and 20p.
Employees are taxed on payments made by their employers over and above the rates in the table.

Employees (including full-time working directors who own 5% or under of the company's shares) earning less than £8,500 per annum including expenses are not taxed on most benefits or perks provided by their employers. In addition to those in the above list, the most valuable non-taxable benefits for this type of employee are private medical insurance and a company car.

Other directors and employees (including full-time working directors), whose total earnings, including expenses, exceed £8,500 per annum, are generally taxed on the actual value of any benefits obtained from their employments. If you fall within this category we have already seen that information about your expense payments and benefits-in-kind is supplied to your tax office annually on a Form P11D.

It is down to you to justify that you are not to be taxed on them. This should not cause you any difficulties where the expenses, such as travelling and entertaining, have genuinely arisen during the performance of the duties of your employment.

The value of some benefits is calculated differently.

(a) Company cars

Generally regarded as the most valuable and sought after benefit, it is measured according to a fixed scale. For cars with an original value up to £19,250 this is determined by their cubic capacity. For more luxurious cars the benefit is governed by price alone. The full scale of benefits for 1993/94 is:

	Age at end of tax year	
Original Market Value of company car	Under 4 years old	4 or more years old
	£	£
Up to £19,250		
1400 cc or less	2,310	1,580
1401 cc to 2000 cc	2,990	2,030
Over 2000 cc	4,800	3,220
£19,251 to £29,000	6,210	4,180
Over £29,000	10,040	6,660

Where the business usage in a tax year is more than 18,000 miles the scale benefit is halved. Where it is under 2,500 miles per annum it is increased to 1½ times the amounts in the above table. The 1½-times rate is also charged on a second company car. Mileage between your home and place of business counts as private, not business usage.

Home-to-work travel in a car made available by an employer is not regarded as private use where:

- The employee has a travelling appointment;

- The employee travels from home to a temporary place of work and the distance travelled is less than the distance between the normal place of work and the temporary place of work;

- Exceptionally, the home qualifies under tax law as a place of work and the employee travels from home to another place of work in the performance of his duties.

There are also circumstances where home-to-work travel in a car provided by an employer is regarded as private use but is ignored for tax purposes. These are where:

- A disabled person is provided with a car from home-to-work travel and there is no other private use;
- A car is provided for home-to-work travel when public transport is disrupted;
- A car is provided for late night journeys from work to home;
- The car is from an employer's car pool and any home-to-work travel is merely incidental to its business use. The car must not be garaged at or near the employee's home overnight.

If it is the company's policy to meet the cost of fuel for private motoring there is an additional taxable benefit. Again it is based on predetermined fixed amounts dependent on the cubic capacity of the company car. For 1993/94 the scale of benefits, incorporating the new and separate scale charge for diesel is:

Cubic Capacity	Petrol	Diesel
	£	£
1400 cc or less	600	550
1401 cc to 2000 cc	760	550
Over 2000 cc	1,130	710

These amounts are reduced by half if you do at least 18,000 miles per annum on business.

From 6 April 1994 there is a new system for working out the tax you will pay on a company car. This is dealt with in the Budget measures supplement at the end of the book.

(b) Mobile telephones

There is also a fixed benefit to cover the private use of a mobile telephone provided by an employer. For 1993/94 an employee will pay Income Tax on the standard amount of £200 for each mobile telephone. This amount can be reduced where the mobile telephone is not available for the full tax year. An employee can escape this tax charge altogether if no private calls are made on the mobile telephone or if the employer is reimbursed for the full cost of the private use. A call is not considered a private call where it is made for business reasons but contains an incidental, non-business element.

(c) Company vans

Also taxable on a fixed amount is an employee to whom a company van is made available for private use, again including travel between home and work. For 1993/94 the taxable benefit is £500 for a van under four years old at the end of the tax year. For older vans the amounts on which you pay tax is reduced to £350. Both fixed benefits also cover the cost of any fuel provided for private motoring. As with company cars, the use of a van from an employer's van pool should not normally give rise to a tax charge. These rules apply to a company van with a design weight up to 3500 kilograms. There is no taxable benefit on the incidental private use of a heavy commercial vehicle with a design weight exceeding 3500 kilograms.

(d) Living accommodation

In some trades it is established practice for the employer to provide living accommodation. This can also be desirable where there is a security risk. No Income Tax liability arises in either sort of situation.

In other circumstances Income Tax is chargeable on the annual value of the property after deducting any rent paid for it. The annual value of property for these purposes is broadly equivalent to the gross rateable value. Estimated rateable values will be used for new properties which do not appear on the domestic rating lists. An additional tax charge must be faced where the accommodation costs more than £75,000. This is worked out by applying the Inland Revenue's official interest rate (see below) at the beginning of the tax year to the excess of the cost price over £75,000.

(e) Beneficial loans

Loans from an employer which are either interest free or where the interest charged by the employer is below a commercial rate can give rise to a taxable benefit. The benefit is calculated by applying the Inland Revenue's official rate of interest to the loan. This is the base lending rate of the major clearing banks rounded to the nearest whole number, plus 1.5%. At the time of going into print the rate is 7.5%. The benefit is reduced by any interest actually paid on the loan. No charge to tax arises where the value of the benefit is less than £300, or where the loan is for a purpose on which the interest would qualify for tax relief (see Chapter 3). The £300 exemption limit is probably most widely used to avoid a tax charge on loans to employees to purchase an annual season ticket.

As there is no higher rate tax relief on mortgage interest, employees who are also top rate taxpayers, with cheap or interest-free mortgage loans from their employers face a further tax charge. At the rate of 15%, the difference between the higher and basic rates of tax, it will be based on the difference between an amount calculated at the official rate of interest on their mortgage advance, where appropriate limited to £30,000, and the interest actually paid on the loan.

(f) Medical insurance
You will be taxed on private medical insurance premiums paid by your employer for you or other members of your family. If you go abroad on business then the cost of medical insurance cover, or actual medical treatment overseas, is not taxable on you as a benefit.

(g) Relocation expenses
An employee who changes his job, or is relocated by his employer, is not taxable on the costs of a relocation package up to £8,000. This limit applies to each job-related move. There are specific definitions for the removal expenses and benefits which qualify for exemption within the monetary limit.

Employee share ownership
No liability to Income Tax is imposed on a director or employee who acquires or disposes of ordinary shares under his employer's Approved Share Option Scheme. An option must be exercised not less than three, or more than ten, years after it is granted, nor under three years after a previous exercise. The gain is measured by the difference between the sale proceeds and the cost of acquiring the shares, and is charged to Capital Gains Tax at the time of disposal. The price payable under the option agreement must not be less than the market value of the shares at the date the option is granted. A number of other requirements must be met by both the employee and the employing company.

Gains from Approved Savings-Related Share option Schemes are free of Income Tax. You must set aside the money to acquire shares in your employer's company through an Approved Savings Scheme. The maximum amount you can contribute is £250 per month. The price at which options can be offered to you cannot be less than 80% of the market value of the shares at the time the options are granted.

Under Profit Sharing Schemes, Trustees are allowed to acquire shares for you each year in your employer's company up to an amount equivalent to 10% of your salary with a minimum limit of £3,000 and a maximum of £8,000. You do not face any Income Tax liability when the shares are set aside for you nor if they are retained by the Trustees of the Scheme for 5 years.

There are other forms of Unapproved Share Option and Share Incentive Schemes as well as Employee Share Ownership Trusts but it is outside the scope of this book to go into these in detail.

Profit-related pay
Profit-related pay is that part of an employee's pay which is linked to the profits of his or her employer. All PRP is free of Income Tax up to the point where PRP is either 20% of pay or £4,000 a year, whichever is lower. This relief is worth as much as £1,000 per annum for a basic rate taxpayer and up to £1,600 annually for a higher rate taxpayer. Your tax relief is passed on to you through your employer's PAYE scheme. Relief only applies to PRP payments made under a scheme registered by an employer with the Inland Revenue.

Payments on termination of employment
It is common practice for an employee to be paid a lump sum on the termination of an employment. If the right to receive the payment arose during the period of employment then it is taxable in full in the same way as other earnings. Otherwise the lump sum payment is either wholly or partly tax free. The occasions when the payments are free of tax are:

(1) Where the employment ceases because of the accidental death, injury or disability of the employee.

(2) Where most of the employee's time was spent working overseas for the employer.

(3) Where the lump sum payment is made at a time other than on death or retirement. The first £30,000 is then tax free. Only the excess of any payment over £30,000 is taxable.

Any statutory redundancy payment you receive, although exempt from tax itself, has to be counted in with any other lump sum payment from your employer in working out the tax due on the lump sum.

National Insurance

Although it is not within the scope if this book to go into National Insurance in detail I cannot pass on to the next chapter without mentioning it briefly. During recent years it has had an ever increasing impact on your salary cheque or pay packet. Although certain allowances and reliefs are deductible in calculating how much Income Tax you pay on your earnings, no similar rules apply for National Insurance purposes. The rate of contribution is applied to your gross earnings. The rates and the earnings levels on which they are calculated are set out in Table 3 at the end of the book.

5

VALUE ADDED TAX

Value Added Tax (VAT) is a tax on supplies of goods and services. Although it normally ends up in the price eventually paid by the final consumer, it is charged and collected all the way along the line, from producer or manufacturer, through wholesaler or distributor, and then on through the retailer, each link in the chain paying a share to Customs and Excise.

It is the responsibility of all businesses to make sure that they not only register for VAT at the right time but also account for and properly pay what they should to Customs and Excise. The tax is, therefore, self-assessed. Checks are carried out from time to time to make sure that no errors or mistakes are being made by businesses.

Rates of tax

The majority of goods and services supplied in the UK are liable to VAT at the standard rate of 17.5%. Domestic fuel and power will have a 'staged' VAT rate of 8%. Both the 8% and 17.5% rates are termed 'positive' rates for VAT purposes. Exports to non-EC countries, books and newspapers and most foods sold in shops are, however, zero rated. Some services in connection with education, health, banking and insurance are exempt from VAT. It is important to realize that zero, as well as 8% and 17.5%, is a rate of tax since the time for deciding whether, and if so when, to register for VAT depends on the amount of taxable supplies made by your business. The turnover from any exempt supplies does not count towards the registration limit.

Registration

If your business is just starting, it is unlikely that you will have to register immediately: only when the value of your taxable supplies reaches £45,000 in a 'rolling' period of 12 months is application compulsory. Before 1 December 1993 the annual turnover limit was £37,600.

It is vital that you do not delay submitting an application for registration as soon as it has to be made. A VAT 1 Form can be obtained form your local VAT office. This has to be completed no later than 30 days from the end of the month when your turnover exceeds the £45,000 limit.

Illustration

A trader commenced in business on 1 May 1993. His turnover between May 1993 and June 1994 was as follows:

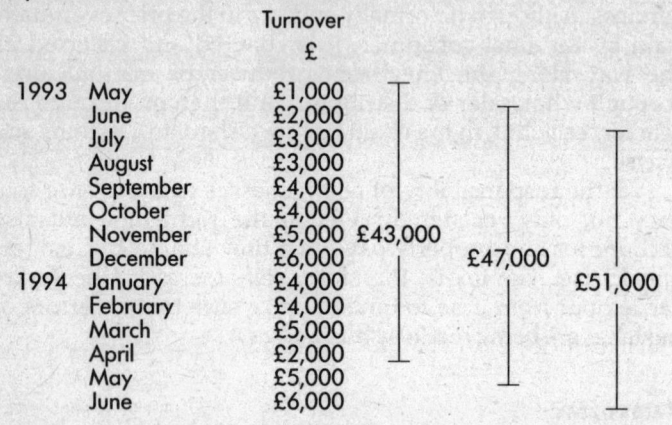

		Turnover £			
1993	May	£1,000			
	June	£2,000			
	July	£3,000			
	August	£3,000			
	September	£4,000			
	October	£4,000			
	November	£5,000	£43,000		
	December	£6,000		£47,000	
1994	January	£4,000			£51,000
	February	£4,000			
	March	£5,000			
	April	£2,000			
	May	£5,000			
	June	£6,000			

As the turnover in the period from 1 May 1993 to 30 April 1994 was less than £45,000, there was then no requirement to register. The 12 month period from 1 June 1993 to 31 May 1994 saw the turnover increase to £47,000. The local VAT office should be advised during June 1994. Registration would usually be effective from 1 July 1994. Had the turnover in May 1994 remained at the same level as April the total turnover for the 'rolling' period of 12 months from the beginning of June 1993 to the end of May 1994 would have remained below the limit requiring registration. However, even if the May 1994 turnover figure was only £2,000, a June 1994 turnover of more than £3,000 would have taken the total turnover for the 12 months ending 30 June 1994 above the compulsory registration limit. Once the registration limit is exceeded, it would only be if the Customs and Excise could be satisfied turnover would remain at an annual level of less than £43,000 that registration could be avoided. This is in line with the limit set for businesses already VAT registered when they are considering deregistration. Up until 30 November 1993 this limit was £36,000.

Sometimes there are benefits in registering even though your turnover does not come up to the compulsory registration limit. Voluntary registrations of this nature are allowed providing that you are, or will be, making some taxable supplies. In this way VAT incurred on your business expenses can be claimed back, including the VAT paid on any assets like computers and printers on hand at the time of registration, as well as on certain costs of starting up your business.

If you are in partnership you must also complete a Form VAT 2 in addition to the VAT 1 Form.

Shortly after you have completed the registration forms and have sent them off, you will receive your registration certificate and a selection of notices and leaflets. These are of a general nature and intended to help you understand the workings of the tax and to assist you in complying with all the rules and regulations. It may be that other leaflets are available which apply to your particular type of business and it is wise to ask your VAT office to send these to you. A list, which includes the leaflets most likely to be of help, is at Table 4 at the end of the book.

New businesses which do not keep an eye on how their turnover is progressing can be caught out by a scaled penalty imposed for not registering when they should. The penalty is calculated as follows:

Registration not more than 9 months late	10%
Registration over 9 months but not more than 18 months late	20%
Registration more than 18 months late	30%

The penalty is based on the tax due for the period beginning on the date when registration is received or liability to be registered is discovered. There is a minimum penalty of £50.

Records and accounting

Output tax is what you are liable for on the supplies you make (outputs) and input tax is on the purchases you receive (inputs). You should keep a copy of the invoice for every supply made by your business. An analysed listing should be maintained along the following lines:

Invoice		Customer	VAT excl Value	VAT	Gross Value
No	Date				
			£	£	£

For your own benefit it is recommended that an additional column is incorporated to show the date when payment is received from your customer.

Similarly, purchase invoices should be analysed in your records and filed by you in such a way that it is possible to trace any item where input tax is claimed to the tax invoice for the purchase. Special care should be taken to make sure tax invoices do not get lost.

Although output tax is usually based on tax invoices issued, input tax can be claimed — if it is more convenient — when purchase invoices are settled.

You will find it best to total your outputs and inputs monthly. You will then be well prepared to bring together the details relating to the periods which correspond with the VAT accounting quarters set for you when you register. A summary of the monthly tax totals can then be noted in a VAT Account which acts as a link between your own records and the VAT Return — Form VAT 100 — which will be sent to you. Very simply, and if your quarters are in line with the calendar quarters, the VAT Account may, for the January to March period, be like this:

VAT Account Period 1 January 1994 to 31 March 1994

	£	£
Output Tax		
January	2,470	
February	2,360	
March	2,520	
Total	£7,350	7,350
Input Tax		
January	910	
February	820	
March	680	
Total	£2,410	2,410
Net amount due		£4,940

Using the figures in your VAT Account and the tax-exclusive values of your outputs and inputs you will be in a position to complete the various boxes on your VAT Return.

When the Return ends up showing an amount of tax due to the Customs and Excise you should send it off with a cheque in settlement. If the VAT claimable on the purchases for the business exceeds the VAT charged on your supplies, the Return will show you are entitled to a repayment. This will be sent to you although it may be subject to verification before you receive the refund.

Input tax

It is only the input tax which is incurred on purchases for your business which can count towards how much is claimed. Sometimes you might incur expenses where the input tax cannot be claimed at all. Among these are costs for business entertaining and on the purchase of a car (unless you are a driving instructor or taxi driver or you trade in new cars. The same applies if your business is that of leasing cars to taxi drivers or driving instructors). You may have other costs which are partly business and partly private, for example, telephone bills. It is then necessary to apportion how much input tax can be claimed as being for business use. Providing this is done in a reasonable manner, Customs and Excise will go along with the method you adopt.

How to treat input tax on motor fuel for cars is also not straightforward since it is difficult to keep detailed records of all business journeys. There are two ways for dealing with this. Either all input tax on motor fuel can be claimed with a fixed scale charge applied to take account of private use, or no input tax at all is claimed on the fuel. As a guide the fixed scale charge is normally the better way if private motoring paid for by the business is more than about 8,000 miles a year. The quarterly fixed scale charges are as follows:

Engine Size	Diesel Scale Charge £	VAT £	Petrol Scale Charge £	VAT £
1400 cc or less	138	20.55	150	22.34
1401 cc to 1999 cc	138	20.55	190	28.30
Over 1999 cc	178	26.51	283	42.18

Input tax on repairs and maintenance of business cars can be claimed whichever way you decide to deal with motor fuel.

Special schemes for retailers

Retailers seldom issue invoices but sell a mixture of both standard and zero-rated goods. Occasionally there may be some sales liable at 8%, for example coal. A number of schemes have therefore been devised so that retailers can calculate their VAT liabilities. If your business falls into this category, you should study the leaflets telling you about the various schemes so that you do not pay too much tax.

Where retailers sell only goods which are liable to the standard rate of 17.5%, the amount of tax included in the gross takings for a period is 7/47. Referred to as the 'VAT fraction', the basis for this calculation is as follows:

		£
Tax exclusive value (say)		100.00
Add: VAT @ 17.5%		17.50
Tax inclusive price		£117.50

The VAT included in the tax inclusive price is therefore:

$$\frac{17.5}{117.5} = \frac{7}{47}$$

For goods liable at 8% the 'VAT fraction' will be 2/27. When retailers are asked for one, they must issue a proper tax invoice for supplies where the value exceeds £100. For supplies below this figure, till receipts may have enough information on them for the appropriate VAT fraction to be applied by customers who, in the course of their business, make retail purchases and want to claim back the input tax suffered.

Helpful schemes for smaller businesses

If your taxable turnover is less than £350,000 per annum you can account for VAT on a basis working just from cash receipts and payments, and, after a year, apply to use the Annual Accounting Scheme — a facility encouraged by the Customs and Excise. Under this arrangement Returns are made at regular annual — as opposed to the usual quarterly — intervals. A VAT assessment is issued in advance for the following year. This is based on the total of the VAT payments in the previous year. The following yearly cycle would be like this:

First Year
Month 1   Estimated assessment issued for the year
Months 4-12 10% of VAT due on the estimated assessment to be paid each month by direct debit.
Second Year
Month 2   VAT Return for the previous year to be filed and the final instalment to be paid, adjusted upwards or downwards to agree the liability for the year.

Since only the one Return has to be completed under this scheme each year, it is likely to appeal to those in business who want to reduce to a bare minimum any prospect of incurring surcharges, penalties or interest.

Partial exemption
This is a complex area which occurs when some supplies made by a business are taxable, whether at the positive or zero rates, and others are exempt. Strictly, the input tax may only be claimed when it relates to taxable supplies, but this is not always so. A relaxation in the rules allows recovery of all claimable input tax if that which relates to the exempt supplies is less than £600 per month on average.

Control visits
Every now and then a Customs and Excise officer will make an appointment to visit you. Initially, he will want a discussion with you and to ask questions about your business. This is followed by an examination of your books and records to make sure that you are keeping proper records and correctly dealing with your quarterly Returns. The officer will draw your attention to any mistakes which he finds you have made and issue an assessment for any underdeclared or overdeclared tax. As a precautionary measure prior to the visit, it is worthwhile carrying out a review of the Returns which you have submitted, since the serious misdeclaration penalty and default interest are likely to be imposed if substantial amounts of tax have been undeclared.

Penalties, surcharges and interest
There are a number of penalties for the unwary and non-compliant trader. Whenever Returns are submitted, the aim should be for the true tax in each and every period to be

declared and paid. Getting it right first time is best for everybody's sake. Errors, although they may be innocent, are always possible. If, when you are preparing a Return for a current period, you find that you have made a mistake in the immediately preceding quarter, you can make an appropriate adjustment without incurring a penalty.

Furthermore, any errors which, taken altogether, involve an amount of tax less than £2,000 can be adjusted in the Return for a current quarter. However, if the total of any errors exceeds £2,000, spotting where they have been made and what they amout to, and owning up, means that the chance of incurring the serious misdeclaration penalty may be avoided. Form VAT652 is available for notifying your VAT office of errors greater than £2,000. Alternatively, details of any errors of this size may be set out in a letter which should be sent together with a payment to correct the overall position. Default interest will be charged when assessments for errors are issued as well as on those where the VAT office has been notified using the form VAT652 or letter procedure.

At the present time the level of the serious misdeclaration penalty is a flat 15% but whether or not it is imposed depends very much upon the correct amount of tax which should have been declared for the quarter.

Failure to pay the proper amount of tax when it is due can lead to the imposition of surcharges. These can range from 2% to 15% if a history of default builds up. Surcharge assessments will, however, seldom be issued unless calculated to exceed £200.

A further type of penalty may also apply if mistakes are persistently made.

Appeals

If you disagree with an officer's assessment or wish to appeal against a penalty or surcharge, you can ask for the matter to be reconsidered by your local VAT office. A review will be carried out by someone more senior than the officer who issued the assessment or penalty. Alternatively, an appeal can be lodged for hearing before an independent VAT Tribunal.

The outcome of appeals depends very much upon the reasons why mistakes were made in the first place. Innocence is not normally accepted as an excuse.

Local VAT offices

The address of your local office can be found in the telephone directory under Customs and Excise. There are various sections within every office dealing with different aspects of the tax. The enquiries section is the one which has most day-to-day contact with businesses. The staff there are able to give help and advice when required. It is however always advisable to obtain any decisions of a technical nature in writing.

Supplies to/from EC countries

There are special rules for these supplies which although they may differ from rules covering exports to, and imports from, countries outside the EC, have been designed to ease the difficulties which businesses have had to face in the past. It is as well to study carefully the leaflet issued by Customs if your business is likely to be involved with such trade.

6

THE SELF-EMPLOYED

You cannot simply choose to be taxed on your earnings as a self-employed person. It is a matter of fact whether you are working on your own account or for someone else as an employee. The concept of self-employment extends to all trades, professions and vocations. You are not self-employed if you are running your business through a company. If you are employed but have some other freelance business activity as well, you will be taxed on these profits as a self-employed person.

The obligations imposed on the taxpayer who is self-employed are more onerous than those which apply to the employee. Proper records must be maintained of all business transactions. At the end of each financial year they are all brought together into an account of the income and expenditure of the business for the past 12 months. Whenever possible a balance sheet should be drawn up showing the assets and liabilities of the business at the year end. It is also better to operate your business through a separate bank account.

Accounts

You can choose the date to which you make up the accounts of your trade or business each year. For this reason it is unlikely that the first accounts will cover a full year's business activities. Thereafter your accounts should continue to be made up to the same date every year although you can alter this where you can show good reason for a change.

Your accounts should be drawn up to show the profit or loss earned in the financial year. This is not usually the simple difference between the cash received and the cash paid out. For example, if you sell to some of your customers on credit there will inevitably be some unpaid invoices at the end of the financial year. Nevertheless, the amount of these outstanding invoices needs to come into your accounts as income for that period. Equally, where amounts are owing to your suppliers at the year-end these must be brought into the accounts as expenses incurred in the year. If your trade is one where you need to keep a stock of raw materials or finished goods, the value of that stock at the year-end must enter your accounts. It will usually be valued at cost or, in the case of redundant or old stock, at realizable value.

Make sure you include in your accounts all the expenses of running your business, If, for example, your wife helps you by taking telephone messages or acting as your part-time assistant or secretary pay her a proper wage for these services. What you pay her can count as an expense in your accounts. She can then set off her personal allowance against her wages. If these are less than £2,912 a year there will be no tax or National Insurance to pay on them. There will be some items of expenditure, such as a car used both privately and in your business, when it will be difficult to differentiate precisely between the private and business elements of the expenditure. Where there is this overlap you should agree the proportion which relates to your business with the Inland Revenue. If you do your office work from home you can include as a deduction in your accounts a proportion of your home expenses, such as light, heat and insurance. Remember that if part of your home is used exclusively for business purposes, then should you come to sell your house the profit on sale attributable to that part will not be exempt from Capital Gains Tax.

Small businesses do not need to send detailed accounts to the Inland Revenue. Simple three-line accounts are sufficient. These should state total turnover, total business purchases and expenses, and the resulting profit or loss. These simplified accounts will be accepted if the total annual turnover of your business is under £15,000. You should still keep proper business accounts and records in order to draw up the annual three-line statement correctly.

Illustration

David Smith runs a successful Art Gallery from rented high street premises. He employs a full-time assistant and his wife keeps his accounts and does his VAT returns as well as acting as part-time secretary.

In August 1992 David spent £1,200 on a desk and chairs. He also traded in his old car for £1,500. In June 1993 he bought a new car for £10,800.

David Smith
Art Gallery

Profit and Loss Account for the year ended 31 July 1993

		£
Sales		116,250

Less: Cost of sales

	£	£
Stock of pictures at 1 August 1992	6,800	
Purchases during the year	62,400	
	69,200	
Less: Stock of pictures at 31 July 1993	7,700	
		61,500
Gross Profit		54,750

Less: Overhead expenses

	£	
Gallery expenses		
Rent and rates	10,500	
Light and heat	670	
Telephone	420	
Insurance	230	
Redecorations	1,200	
		13,020
Assistant's salary and pension contribution		12,050
Wife's salary		2,100
Postage and stationery		180
Advertising		340
Travelling		460
Entertaining		220
Trade books and magazines		110
Trade subscription		140
Car expenses		
Road Fund Licence and Insurance	380	
Petrol and oil	650	
Repairs and servicing	120	
	1,150	
Business proportion 75%		862
Use of home as office ($1/7 \times 560$)		80
Home telephone (25%)		90
Provision for bad debts ($10\% \times 2,500$)		250
Donations to charity (non-business)		60
Miscellaneous expenses		108
		30,070
Profit for the year		£24,680

Business Economic Notes

Business Economic Notes are published from time to time by the Inland Revenue. They give information on the finance and business background of particular trades and professions and are used in tax offices when traders' business accounts are examined. The notes are based primarily on research into publicly available material such as the trade press and specialist books of reference. They have also been discussed with some or all of the principal trade and professional associations. However, they are not intended to be definitive or comprehensive descriptions of particular trades or professions. Copies of the Business Economic Notes published so far can be obtained from the Inland Revenue Reference Room, at Somerset House in London. There is a small fee to pay.

Computation of profits

It does not follow that the profit shown by your business accounts is the same as the one on which you pay tax. This is because some items of expenditure are specifically not deductible in computing your taxable business profits. Types of expenditure which come into this category are business entertainment, non-business charitable donations, general provisions and reserves, professional costs related to capital expenditure, and the cost of items of a capital, as opposed to revenue, nature.

Illustration

Although David Smith's accounts for the year to 31 July 1993 show a profit of £24,680 his taxable profits are £25,210, as follows:

	£	£
Profit as per accounts		24,680
Add Disallowable expenses:		
General provision for bad debts	250	
Entertainment	220	
Donations	60	
		530
Profit as adjusted for tax purposes		£25,210

Assessment of profits

Your tax assessment is based on the profits for the accounting year which ended in the preceding year of assessment. For example, the profits from David Smith's Art Gallery for the year to 31 July 1993 will be taxed in 1994/95. The tax will be payable in two equal instalments on 1 January and 1 July 1995.

Where a new trade or business is set up, the assessments for more than one tax year are governed by the results for the first period of trading.

Illustration

Had David Smith only started his Art Gallery on 1 August 1992 his results for the year to 31 July 1993 would have formed the basis of his assessment for the first three years, as follows:

1992/93	
Profits earned in year of assessment —	
8/12 × profits in year to 31 July 1993	£16,806
1993/94	
Profits of first year's trading —	
year to 31 July 1993	£25,210
1994/95	
Profits shown by accounts ending in the preceding year of assessment —	
year to 31 July 1993	£25,210

Where it is advantageous the taxpayer can elect that the assessments for both the second and third years, but not only one of them, be adjusted to the actual profits earned in those years.

If you ever set up in business choose carefully the date to mark the end of your accounting year. To save Tax during the early stages of a new business it has usually been sensible to select a date shortly after 5 April, such as the end of each April or May. However, with the move over to the current year basis of assessment from 1997/98 (see Chapter 17) different considerations will apply.

Where a business ceases to function, the assessment for the final year will be based on the profits from 6 April up to the date of cessation. The Inland Revenue has the option to adjust the assessments for the two years, but not only one of them, prior to the year in which cessation takes place. These assessments are revised to the actual profits earned in those years where this is to the Inland Revenue's advantage.

Capital allowances

Although you cannot deduct expenditure on items of a capital nature directly from your business profits, you do receive allowances for them. They are known as capital allowances. Generally, the total allowances due for a year of assessment are measured by the capital transactions of your business in the accounting year which forms the basis of the assessment.

Expenditure on machinery, equipment, motor vans, fixtures and fittings, and motor cars qualifies for a writing-down allowance of 25% per annum, commencing with the year of purchase. Thereafter the annual allowance of 25% is calculated on the balance after deduction of previous allowances. For cars costing more than £12,000 there is a maximum allowance of £3,000 per annum.

Expenditure on plant and machinery, excluding cars and certain other assets, incurred by businesses in the twelve-month period from the beginning of November 1992 to the end of October 1993 attracted a 40% first year allowance. This new allowance was given instead of the 25% writing down allowance otherwise available in the year when expenditure is incurred. The balance of expenditure will continue to be written down in subsequent years on the reducing balance basis at a rate of 25% per annum.

A separate 'pool' of expenditure must be maintained for each of these different categories, as follows:

(1) Plant and equipment, including motor vans and lorries
(2) Cars costing up to £12,000
(3) Each car bought for over £12,000
(4) Each asset used for both personal and business use
(5) Each asset with a short life expectancy.

Where an asset on which capital allowances have been given is sold, such as David Smith's old car, the proceeds of sale must come into the computation of capital allowances. This can sometimes lead to a further allowance where an asset is sold for less than its written-down value for tax purposes. Alternatively, if it fetches an amount greater than its written-down value this can often mean that part of the allowances already given need to be withdrawn. These adjustments are respectively referred to as balancing allowances and balancing charges.

Illustration

David Smith's claim to capital allowances for 1994/95, based on his capital expenditure in the year to 31 July 1993, is:

	Pool £	Car with Private Use £
Written down values brought forward from 1993/94	800	1,800
Sale proceeds of car		1,500
Balancing allowance		300
Additions in the year:		
Desk and chairs	1,200	
New car		10,800
	2,000	
Allowances due:		
Writing down — 25%	500	2,700
Carried forward to 1995/96	£1,500	£8,100
Summary of allowances:		
Writing down		3,200
Balancing		300
		3,500
Less: 25% private use of car		750
1994/95 Capital allowances		£2,750

Expenditure on plant and machinery can only qualify for capital allowances for a particular chargeable period if it is notified to the Inspector of Taxes within two years from the end of that period. Where the time limit is not met capital allowances on the expenditure can be claimed for a later period which is still in date. It will be sufficient for these purposes if the capital expenditure is included as part of the normal annual tax computation for your business. These rules apply to expenditure not notified to your Inspector of Taxes before 30 November 1993.

Losses

Most businesses cannot escape going through a bad spell at some stage in their existence. Where the results of the business for the year show a loss you will be able to claim tax relief on the loss as increased by the amount of any claim to capital allowances. The overall loss is set against your other taxable income for the same year – which will include the

LOSSES 55

profits from your business for the previous accounting year. Any unused part of the loss can then be set against your taxable income in the subsequent year. The balance of the loss which is left over must be carried forward to be set against the profits from the same business in later years.

There is a set procedure for setting off the loss. It must first of all reduce your other earned income for the year, then your investment income. Loss relief against other income must be claimed by sending an election to your tax office within two years after the end of the tax year in which it arises.

Illustration

A trader suffered a loss of £6,000 in his business for the year ended 31 March 1994. His claim to capital allowances for the year is £1,500. His own investment income for 1993/94 was £1,700.

In the previous year to 31 March 1993 the trader's taxable profits were £4,000.

The total business loss is:

	£
Trading loss	6,000
Capital allowances	1,500
	£7,500

This is set off as follows:

Profits for the year to 31 March 1993 – taxed in 1993/94	4,000
Investment income	1,700
1993/94 Loss relief claim	£5,700

The unrelieved loss of £1,800 can either be set off against the trader's income in 1994/95 or carried forward against future profits from the same business in later years.

If the end of your financial year does not coincide with the tax year, your loss should be split on a time basis between the tax years into which it falls.

Illustration

A trader incurred a loss of £4,200 in his business in the year to 31 October 1993. This will be apportioned as follows:

		£
1992/93:	5/12 × £4,200	1,750
1993/94:	7/12 × £4,200	2,450
		£4,200

Alternatively, where the loss arises in an established business the Inland Revenue will usually allocate the loss to the tax year in which the financial year ends.

Otherwise you can claim to offset a trading loss against capital gains. The time limit for making the claim is the same as that for setting off a business loss against your other income. The claim is for relief on the amount of the trading loss which cannot be set against your other income in the year or on which tax relief has already been allowed in some other way. The maximum loss eligible for relief against capital gains is equivalent to the amount on which you would be chargeable to Capital Gains Tax before deducting the annual exemption limit (see Chapter 11). It is not possible to make a partial claim. As a result, it is possible that personal allowances may be wasted as well as the annual exemption for Capital Gains Tax.

There is an alternative form of loss relief available for new businesses. It allows losses incurred during the first four years of assessment to be set against your income in the three years prior to that in which the loss arises. Relief is first of all given against your income for the earliest year. For example, if you started out in business during 1993/94 and incur a loss in the first period of trading, the proportion attributable to the tax year 1993/94 can be set off against your income in 1990/91, 1991/92 and 1992/93, starting with 1990/91. The first of these tax years was before the start of Independent Taxation. If you were married the Income Tax repayable will be worked out by setting the loss firstly against your other income in this first year followed by your spouse's earned and investment income in that order.

Frequently it is necessary to incur expenditure on a new business venture before it starts to trade. Any such expenditure incurred within five years prior to the commencement of trade is treated as a separate loss sustained in the tax year in which trading began.

There is also a special form of loss relief for those businesses which incur a loss in their final period of trading. As the business has ceased there cannot be any future profits against which the loss might be relieved. Therefore, you are allowed to set a loss arising in the final 12 months of trading against the profits from the same business in the three preceding years beginning with the profits of the latest year and working backwards.

Illustration

A trader retired from business on 30 November 1993. Apart from the final 8 months when he lost £21,000 his business had always been successful. His profits and the assessments based on these were as follows:

Accounting Year	Taxable Profits £	Year of Assessment
Year ended 31 March 1990	17,000	1990/91
" " " 1991	15,000	1991/92
" " " 1992	6,000	1992/93
" " " 1993	8,000	1993/94

The assessment in the final year, 1993/94, will be reduced to nil. Unused losses of £13,000 are left over which can be set off as follows:

1992/93	6,000	leaving nil taxable profits
1991/92	7,000	reducing the taxable profits to £8,000
	£13,000	

The Enterprise Allowance

The Enterprise Allowance is a weekly payment for one year to individuals leaving the unemployment register to set up in business. The allowance is not included in the takings of the recipient's business, although it is chargeable to Income Tax.

National Insurance

Like any employee you must pay National Insurance contributions if you are self-employed. There are two rates. Class 2 is a weekly flat rate and Class 4 is based on a percentage of your business profits. If your earnings are below a specified limit you can be exempted from payment of Class 2 contributions. Table 3 at the end of the book sets out the rates for both Classes.

Half the amount of your Class 4 National Insurance contributions is allowed as a deduction in calculating your total income for each tax year, as follows:

Illustration

A trader's taxable profits after capital allowances for the year ended 30 September 1992 were £16,200. The Class 4 deduction from total income for 1993/94 is:

$$£16,200 - £6,340 = £9,860 \times 6.3\% \times \frac{1}{2} = £310$$

Special situations

In the space available it has only been possible for me to paint a general picture of the way in which business profits are taxed. If you are a Lloyds underwriter, farmer, writer, subcontractor in the construction industry or in partnership, you should be aware that there are special rules which apply in calculating the tax on the profits from your trade or profession. In these and other situations it is advisable to seek professional assistance.

The letting of holiday accommodation in the UK is treated as a trade. The accommodation has to be furnished residential property which is available for renting by the public as holiday accommodation for at least 140 days during each tax year. It must actually be let for a minimum of 70 days. There are other requirements which also need to be satisfied. Capital gains on disposals of holiday accommodation falling within these rules qualify for the replacement and retirement reliefs which apply to business assets as well as the new re-investment relief (see Chapter 11).

7

PERSONAL PENSIONS

Wherever possible I imagine you will want to avoid a drop in your living standards when you come to retire. When you can afford to do so, you should start contributing towards a pension to supplement the benefits you will receive from the State. Many employers operate their own Company Pension Scheme. If you are in employment you will probably be able to join your employer's scheme. Some employers do not require their employees to make any contributions towards their benefits on retirement. In other cases employees must set aside varying percentages of their annual salary in addition to the amounts that their employers pay into their schemes each year. The maximum amount you can contribute is 15% of your salary. It is highly likely that your contributions will be much lower than this limit. You can use the remainder of your allowance by paying premiums into your own free standing Additional Voluntary Contributions Scheme.

If your employer has not set up his own scheme for his employees or you are self-employed you will need to make your own pension arrangements. You will do this by taking out a Personal Pension Plan. These are generally available from Insurance Companies, Banks and Building Societies.

Eligible individuals

You can take out a personal pension plan if you are either self-employed or in employment. You can even choose to opt out of your employer's own company scheme and take out a personal pension plan instead. Your employer can make contributions into your personal pension plan in addition to the amount of premiums you choose to pay into the plan.

You can also use a personal pension plan to opt out of the State Earnings-Related Pension Scheme (SERPS). The Department of Social Security will then pay the difference between the full and reduced rates of National Insurance Contributions into your personal pension scheme. Opting out of SERPS does not affect your entitlement to the basic National Insurance Pension.

Benefits on retirement

When you start making regular monthly or annual contributions into a personal pension plan do remember you cannot benefit from the funds building up in your plan until you come to retire and draw your pension. Throughout this period your contributions will be invested in a tax-free fund. As we will see later on in this chapter you will also receive tax relief on your premiums. You benefit from a further tax concession on retirement when 25% of the value of the fund built up in your personal pension plan can be paid to you as a tax-free lump sum. The remainder of your fund must be used to provide a pension which will be payable throughout the rest of your life. You can even arrange for this to be paid for a minimum guaranteed period, usually five years, should you die within this period. It is also possible to provide for a widow's pension if you die before your wife. As we will see in Chapter 9 the pension you eventually come to draw from your scheme is taxable.

The tax-free lump sum and pension can be taken at any time between the ages of 50 and 75. The Inland Revenue has approved earlier retirement ages of 30, 35, 40 or 45 for some professions and occupations, particularly in professional sport; for example, footballers can retire at age 35 and take maximum benefits. Those benefits within your plan which were purchased through opting out of SERPS cannot be drawn until you reach normal state retirement age.

If unfortunately you die before retirement a lump sum, depending on the terms of your particular plan, will probably be refundable. This can be paid out to beneficiaries nominated by you during your lifetime or, alternatively, to your executors. Any lump sum payable is free of all taxes.

Tax relief on premiums

If you are in employment your premiums can be paid after deduction of tax at the basic rate. If you are liable to tax at the higher rate of 40%, you will need to tell your tax office about your personal pension plan so that the extra tax relief on your premiums over and above that due at the basic rate can be allowed in your code number.

If you are self-employed the premiums you pay are allowed as a deduction from your profits. The maximum amount you can contribute each year is expressed as a percentage of your earnings and depends on your age. For this purpose your earnings are your annual taxable business profits as reduced by capital allowances and any losses. There is a maximum earnings limit on which the percentage limit can be calculated. For 1993/94 this is £75,000. It is to increase each year in line with the movement in the Retail Prices Index. The contribution limits are as follows:

Age at Start of Tax Year	Percentage Limit of Earnings %
Under 36	17½
36–45	20
46–50	25
51–55	30
56–60	35
Over 60	40

Up to 5% of your annual profits can be paid into a policy providing for the payment of a lump sum to your dependants in the event of your death before the age of 75. Premiums paid into such a policy count as part of the maximum permissible limits set out above.

Where you do not pay premiums up to the maximum permissible amount in any year the shortfall can be carried forward for up to six years. Relief outstanding for earlier years is used up before that still available for later years.

Illustration

A trader has been in business for many years. Since 1989/90 he has not been making the maximum contributions towards his pension, as follows:

Tax Year	Premiums Paid £	Maximum Permissible £	Shortfall £
1989/90	800	2,275	1,475
1990/91	900	1,400	500
1991/92	900	1,100	200
1992/93	1,800	3,000	1,200

During 1993/94 he paid premiums of £3,400; the maximum permissible premium limit for the year was only £1,000. Nevertheless relief will be given for £3,400, as follows:

	£	£
Premium limit for 1993/94		1,000
Unused relief:		
1989/90	1,475	
1990/91	500	
1991/92	200	
1992/93 (part)	225	
		2,400
1993/94 Pension premium relief		£3,400

Premiums paid in the year can either be deducted from your taxable profits in the year of payment, or alternatively you can elect for them to be treated as if paid in the preceding year providing you do not exceed the contribution limit for the earlier year.

Retirement annuities

Personal pension schemes have been around since the beginning of July 1988. Up to that date the self-employed and employees who were not members of their employer's own pension schemes could take out retirement annuities. No new retirement annuities may now be taken out although you can continue to pay regular and single premiums into existing contracts. Retirement annuities differ from personal pension plans in a number of ways:

Employers are not allowed to make contributions into them.

Although there is no maximum earnings limit on which premiums may be paid, the contribution limits are not so generous:

Age at Start of Tax Year	Percentage Limit of Earnings %
Under 51	17½
51–55	20
56–60	22½
Over 60	27½

You cannot draw your benefits before age 60.

The method of calculating the maximum amount of the tax-free lump sum on retirement is more generous.

Waiver of Premium benefits

For the payment of an additional premium within the overall percentage limits – typically between 2% and 3% of pension premiums – an individual can go a long way towards providing for the future security of his or her family. This extra premium also attracts tax relief at the individual's highest rate of tax.

In return the insurance company undertakes, in the event of ill health, to continue contributing to the individual's pension plan and to maintain full bonuses/benefits.

Personal pension planning

If you are still contributing into a retirement annuity you will often have to decide between continuing with this policy or instead opting to take out a personal pension plan. Where your salary or profits fall short of the earnings 'cap' of £75,000 you should consider contributing as much as you can into an existing retirement annuity as well as taking advantage of the higher contribution limits for personal pensions.

Illustration

A businessman aged 44, earns £54,000 per annum. He has an existing retirement annuity and pays premiums of £5,200 each year.

His maximum contribution limits are:

(1) Into his retirement annuity – £9,450 (17½% × £54,000)

(2) Into a personal pension – £10,800 (20% × £54,000)

He can pay either:

(a) A further £4,250 into his retirement annuity and contribute £1,350 into a personal pension, or

(b) A premium of £5,600 into a personal pension.

If you earn more than the amounts in the following table you should consider paying the maximum premiums into your retirement annuity.

Age at 6 April 1993	Earnings £
Under 36	75,000
36–45	85,714
46–50	107,142
51–55	112,500
56–60	116,667
Over 60	109,090

Illustration

A businessman aged 48, earns £110,000 per annum. He has an existing retirement annuity and contributes £12,000 each year.

His maximum contribution limits are:

(1) Into his retirement annuity — £19,250 (17½% × £110,000)

(2) Into a personal pension — £18,750 (25% × £75,000)

He can either contribute:

(a) A further £7,250 into his retirement annuity, or

(b) A premium into a personal pension plan. If he chooses to do so the total additional contributions he can make into the new personal pension and his existing retirement annuity between them are £6,750.

If your earnings are below the amounts in the above table you should again contribute the maximum amount into your existing retirement annuity and top this up by paying a further premium into a personal pension plan.

Illustration

A businessman aged 57, earns £84,000 per annum. He has a retirement annuity and pays premiums of £13,000 annually.

His maximum contribution limits are:

(1) Into his retirement annuity — £18,900 (22½% × £84,000)

(2) Into a personal pension — £26,250 (35% × £75,000)

He can either contribute:

(a) A further £5,900 into his retirement annuity and pay a personal pension premium of £7,350, or

(b) An amount of £13,250 into a personal pension.

8

INVESTMENT INCOME

Most of you will at some time or other need to look into the various types of investment on offer. Perhaps you will be looking to find a suitable home for regular savings or to invest a more substantial amount such as an inheritance or a lump sum on retirement. Investment or unearned income is that which does not depend on your active involvement or physical effort in some business or trade. Bank or building society interest, dividends on shares or unit trust holdings, rents, income from a trust and interest on government stocks are all investment income.

Tax-free income

The most widely known investments where the return is free of both Income Tax and Capital Gains Tax are some of those available from the Department of National Savings. They are:

- Fixed Interest and Index-linked Savings Certificates
- Yearly Savings Plan
- Premium Bond Prizes
- First £70 of annual interest on a National Savings Bank Ordinary Account.

Apart from interest on any National Savings Bank account, no details of these need to be shown on your annual Income Tax Return.

Rental income

If you own a flat, house, shop or some other property which you have let out to tenants you must show the rents and expenses on your Tax Return. The Income Tax payable on your net rental income is due on 1 January each year. For example, the tax payable for 1993/94 was due on 1 January 1994. You may well ask how the right amount of tax payable can be calculated when the exact rental income is not known. The answer is that the Inspector of Taxes issues a provisional assessment based on the agreed income for the previous year. This is adjusted when the current year's income is ascertained.

Apart from expenditure of a capital nature, such as that on structural alterations or improvements, the general running costs of a property can be set against rental income.

Illustration

	£	£
Rent receivable from letting a house		10,800
Less: Expenses		
Water rates	78	
Building insurance	140	
Redecorating two bedrooms	700	
Repairs to washing machine	60	
Agents fees for collecting rent	1,242	
Garden maintenance	260	2,480
1993/94 Net rental income		£8,320

If you are letting a furnished property you can claim an additional deduction to cover the cost of wear and tear to furnishings and fittings. This allowance is based on 10% of the rent less the amount of the water rates. If the property in the preceding illustration is let furnished this allowance would be £1,072, as follows:

Illustration

	£
Rent receivable	10,800
Less: Water rates	78
	£10,722
Wear and tear allowance: 10%	£1,072

The rules dealing with the taxation of premiums on leases and the situations where losses arise on the letting of properties are more complicated and outside the scope of this book.

If your annual gross rental income is less than £15,000 you need only send a simple three-line statement to the Inland Revenue. This should state your gross rents, total property expenses and the resulting profit or loss.

Rent a room

Income from the furnished letting of spare rooms in your home is tax-free providing the annual gross rents do not exceed £3,250 per annum. The space you let out must be in your only or main home. This can be a house, flat, caravan or even a houseboat. You can choose to opt out of the special form of relief. You will then be taxed under the normal rules dealing with income from furnished lettings. If, for example, there was a loss on the letting which could be set against other income then it would pay you to make the opt-out election. It has to be made within one year of the end of the tax year concerned. The same timetable applies for withdrawing an election already in force.

If your annual gross rents are more than £3,250 then you can pay tax on the excess gross rents, without any relief for expenses, or under the rules for taxing furnished lettings income.

Illustration
A basic-rate taxpayer lets a room in his house for £4,000 per annum. The expenses which can be set against the income total £1,400. Under the rent-a-room relief the taxpayer's Income Tax liability is £187.50 (£4,000-£3,250) × 25%. Alternatively, under the normal rules, the tax liability would total £650 (£4,000-£1,400) × 25%.

It is necessary to make an election if you want to adopt the simple method of paying Income Tax on the gross rents over £3,250 per annum. The time limit for either making or withdrawing such an election is again within one year of the end of the tax year to which it applies.

Where more than one individual is entitled to income under the rent-a-room scheme the £3,250 limit is halved. Each lessor's exempt amount is then £1,625. This rule means that a married couple taking in lodgers should be able to arrange their affairs in such a way that the letting income is divisible between them (each spouse will then have a limit of £1,625); or goes wholly to either husband or wife (in which case either spouse will be due the full £3,250 limit).

Dividends and interest
The tables below set out the types of investment where the dividends and interest are paid to the investor after deduction of Income Tax, together with those where no such deduction is made.

Tax credit of 20%
Dividends on shares
Income distributions on unit trust holdings

Tax deducted at the basic rate
Building society interest
Interest on British government stocks
Bank deposit interest

Interest not taxed at source
National Savings Bank ordinary and investment accounts
National Savings Income and Capital Bonds
National Savings First Option Bonds
National Savings Pensioners' Guaranteed Income Bonds
Single deposits over £50,000 for a minimum period of 7 days
Deposits with non-UK branches of banks and building societies

As is illustrated in the first of the above tables the rate of tax credit on dividends paid by UK companies and Unit Trusts is now at the lower rate of 20%. This rate is based on the gross equivalent of the dividend and tax credit attaching to it. Your dividend income is treated as the top part of your taxable income. Non-taxpayers will only be able to claim repayment of Income Tax at 20% on their dividends. For individuals who are liable to Income Tax at the lower rate the tax credit of 20% will match their exact liability. Taxpayers who are liable at the basic rate of 25%, but not the top rate, will not face any further tax charge on their dividend income. Individuals who are liable at the higher 40% rate will be required to pay Income Tax of a further 20% each year to the extent that their dividend income falls above the annual threshold of the basic rate band.

Illustrations

1. An individual receives dividends, including the tax credit, of £600 for 1993/94. His other income, after allowances and reliefs, comes to £3,000. He pays tax for the year as follows:

On the first	£2,500 @ 20%
On the next	£500 @ 25%
On his dividends of	£600 @ 20%

2. Another individual banks dividends of £7,000, including the tax credit, during 1993/94. From other sources he receives income of £19,500 after allowances and reliefs. His tax charge is worked out as follows:

On the first	£2,500 @ 20%
On the next	£17,000 @ 25%
On his dividends of	£4,200 @ 20%
On the final	£2,800 @ 40%

The £4,200 slice of dividend income attracts tax at the rate of 20% as it falls within the limit of income of £23,700 taxed at the lower and basic rates.

Many people mistakenly assume – because the dividends and interest mentioned in the top two tables are paid after tax has been deducted – that they need not be reported on their annual Tax Return. This misunderstanding is most particularly associated with building society interest. Whatever the amount of your dividends and interest these details must be shown on your Tax Return. The size of this income may be such as to give rise to a liability to tax at the higher rate.

Individuals not liable to tax can arrange to receive their interest gross. This is done by completing special forms which are available at Banks, Building Societies, Post Offices and Tax Offices throughout the country. Individual savers who are not liable to tax, but receive interest from which tax has been deducted, can claim repayment from the Inland Revenue. These measures benefit non-earning married women, pensioners, children and other individuals not liable to Income Tax who choose to invest their savings in Banks and Building Societies.

Interest on the various National Savings bonds or accounts in the final table above is taxed in a special way similar to the income or profits from self-employment. When an account has been in existence for at least three years the interest earned in a tax year is the amount on which tax is paid in the following year. However, there are special rules for determining the interest which is taxable – not only in the early years after a new account is opened, but also in the final years before one is closed.

Illustration

A National Savings Bank investment account was opened in July 1991. The interest received and taxable amounts are:

| *Interest Received* | | Tax | Interest | |
| Date | Amount | Year | Taxable | Comments |
	£		£	
Dec 1991	400	1991/92	400	Interest received in the tax year
Dec 1992	900	1992/93	900	Actual interest in the year
Dec 1993	750	1993/94	900	Interest for the previous tax year

The taxpayer can elect for the interest taxable in the third year – 1993/94 – to be adjusted to the actual interest received in the year. In the above illustration the taxpayer would exercise this option and the taxable amount would be reduced to £750.

Illustration

A National Savings Bank Investment Account is closed in August 1993. The interest credited in the final years and the amounts taxable are:

| *Interest Received* | | Tax | Interest | |
| Date | Amount | Year | Taxable | Comments |
	£		£	
Dec 1991	800	1991/92	825	Interest received in the previous year
Dec 1992	650	1992/93	800	Previous year's interest
Aug 1993	400	1993/94	400	Actual interest received in the year.

The Inland Revenue can alter the amount of the assessment in the penultimate year – 1992/93 – to the actual interest received in the year. Clearly in the above illustration this would not be to their advantage as it would reduce the interest taxable from £800 to £650.

As with income from property, Income Tax on untaxed interest is payable on each 1 January.

Accrued income

Interest on fixed-rate investments is treated as accruing on a day-to-day basis between payment dates. On a sale the vendor is charged to Income Tax on the accrued interest from the previous payment date to the date of the transaction. The purchaser is allowed to deduct this amount from the interest which he receives on the following payment date. These arrangements cover both fixed and variable-rate stocks and bonds, including those issued by governments, companies and local authorities. The arrangements will not affect you if the nominal value of your securities is under £5,000.

Illustration

The interest on a holding of 12% Treasury Stock 1995 is payable on each 25 January and 25 July. The half-yearly interest on a holding of £20,000, sold for settlement on 8 May 1993, is £1,200.

Accrued proportion = $^{103}/_{181}$ × £1,200 = £682.87

Single premium bonds

Guaranteed income bonds and investment bonds offered by most insurance companies fall within this category. A lump sum premium is paid at the outset. The investor can usually either draw an income from the bond or leave it untouched until it is cashed. No tax relief is due on the single premium. The proceeds of a bond are not liable to Capital Gains Tax or Income Tax at the basic rate. There can be a liability to tax at the higher rate of 40% on the profit element, depending on the investor's income in the tax year the bond is encashed. The method of calculating the additional Income Tax due on the gain involves a number of stages.

Tax-Exempt Special Savings Accounts

You can invest in a Tax-Exempt Special Savings Account if you are over 18 and resident in the UK. A TESSA is a Savings Scheme with a Bank or Building Society where the interest is tax free. Each individual is only allowed one TESSA.

Husbands and wives are treated separately so they can each start up their own TESSA. The account must run for a full five years. The freedom from Income Tax on the interest will be lost if any part of the capital is withdrawn during the five year investment period.

As TESSAs are primarily aimed to encourage the small saver the investment limit is relatively modest. Up to £9,000 may be invested over the five year period. In the first year the maximum savings limit is £3,000. This reduces to £1,800 in each subsequent year but the overall limit of £9,000 must not be exceeded. Individuals can use a TESSA to make regular monthly savings or to deposit lump sums as and when they can. For example, both the following savings patterns are within the rules:

Year	Amount Invested £	£
1	3,000	2,200
2	1,800	1,800
3	1,800	None
4	1,800	1,500
5	600	1,800
	£9,000	£7,300

Investors can withdraw interest as it arises during the investment period. Up to the full amount of interest which has been credited to the account can be paid out at any time. However, an amount equivalent to the basic rate of Income Tax on the withdrawal must be retained within the TESSA. The Income Tax left in the account can be withdrawn in full at the end of the five-year period. At that time a TESSA will cease to be a tax-exempt fund and any further interest credited to the account will be taxable in the normal way.

If an investor dies during the period when the account is tax free, it comes to an end but none of the tax benefits up to that time are lost.

Your Bank or Building Society will deal with all the paperwork required by the Inland Revenue. You will not need to mention the tax-free interest on your TESSA in your annual Tax Return.

Personal Equity Plans

Personal Equity Plans (PEPs) are a tax-free way of investing in shares. Any dividends you receive on your investments are exempt from Income Tax. There is no Capital Gains Tax to pay on profits made on selling shares within the plan. You do not have to report your dividend income and capital gains to the Inland Revenue on your annual Tax Return.

You can set up a plan so long as you are over 18 and resident in the UK for tax purposes. The maximum amount you can invest each tax year in a PEP is £6,000. Husbands and wives are treated individually so they are both allowed to set up their own plans each year within the maximum investment limit. There are plans which cater for either lump sum investments or regular monthly contributions.

The same plan can invest in shares, investment trusts and unit trusts. The share investments can be either in ordinary shares of UK companies quoted on the UK Stock Exchange or dealt with on the Unlisted Securities Market, or comparable shares of companies incorporated in another EC Member State whose shares are officially listed on a recognized Stock Exchange in the European Community. You can invest up to £1500 of your annual subscription limit in a trust which does not have at least 50% of its own investments in UK or EC companies. Such trusts must, however, hold at least half of their assets in ordinary shares. You can also subscribe for new issue shares such as government privatizations, and transfer them into a PEP. This must be done within 42 days from the time they are allotted to you. There is no limit on the amount of cash that can be held in a plan. All interest is tax free providing the cash is eventually invested in shares or unit trusts.

In addition to the normal investment limit of £6,000 in a general PEP you can put up to £3,000 each tax year in a PEP which, in turn, invests in the shares of a single company. Shares acquired by members of an Approved All Employee Scheme can be transferred direct to a single company PEP, subject, of course, to the £3,000 limit. The transfer must be made within six weeks from the end of the qualifying period to avoid a liability to Capital Gains Tax.

To set up a PEP you will need to use a plan manager. These are individuals or companies specifically authorized to make investments on your behalf and must be approved by the Inland Revenue. You are the owner of the shares, unit trusts or investment trusts but they are held for you by the plan manager who also deals with all other aspects of the administration of your plan, including the claims for tax reliefs and exemptions to the Inland Revenue.

There are no Income Tax or Capital Gains Tax penalties on withdrawing from or closing down a plan.

Friendly Societies
All individuals, including children under 18, can invest up to £200 per annum in a tax-exempt savings plan with a Friendly Society. A family with two children can now save as much as £800 per annum through this type of investment.

Business Expansion Scheme
The Business Expansion Scheme ended on 31 December 1993. Under the Scheme, tax relief was granted on minority investments in trading companies or companies involved in letting residential housing under the assured-tenancy rules. The maximum amount that an individual could invest in additional ordinary shares in new or established qualifying companies whose shares are not quoted on a recognized stock exchange or dealt in on the Unlisted Securities Market was £40,000 per year. The minimum investment limit was £500 per annum. For a married couple living together, these limits applied to them separately. The income tax relief is given by deducting the cost of shares subscribed for from the investor's total income in the year during which they are issued. Investors can claim relief on up to one half of the cost of investments made in the first half of a tax year against income of the previous tax year. The carry-back is limited to a maximum of £5,000. The balance of the relief is allowed in the year during which the investments were actually made. If Business Expansion Scheme investments are disposed of within five years the tax relief can be reduced or withdrawn.

Enterprise Investment Scheme
The Enterprise Investment Scheme applies to shares issued on or after 1 January 1994. The Chancellor's aims are:

- To provide a targeted incentive for new equity investment in unquoted trading companies which will help overcome the problems faced by such companies in raising small amounts of equity finance;
- To encourage outside investors, who introduce finance and expertise to a company, by enabling them to take an active part in the management of the company as paid directors without losing entitlement to relief.

The new Scheme provides Income Tax relief at 20% on qualifying investments up to £100,000 in any tax year. For 1993/94 a limit of £40,000 will apply to an individual's combined investments under both the Business Expansion and the new Enterprise Investment Schemes. Any gain on the disposal of qualifying shares under the new scheme will be exempt from Capital Gains Tax providing the tax relief has not been withdrawn. Investors will be allowed either Income Tax or Capital Gains Tax relief for losses made on the disposal of qualifying shares. All shares in a qualifying company must be held for at least five years. Investors previously unconnected with a qualifying company or its trade can become directors whilst still qualifying for relief on their investment. Relief on up to one-half of the amount that an individual invests between 6 April and 5 October in any tax year can be carried back to the previous tax year, subject to a maximum limit of £15,000.

Qualifying companies are unquoted trading companies which carry on a qualifying activity for a minimum of three years. They will be able to raise up to £1 million a year through the scheme. The new scheme extends to companies which are trading in the United Kingdom whether or not they are incorporated and resident here. Companies investing in private rented housing will be outside the scheme.

Joint income

Many married couples have Bank or Building Society accounts, Unit Trust Holdings or other share investments, or property held in their joint names. They are then treated as if they own the account or asset equally and each will have to pay Income Tax on half the annual income. Alternatively, if capital invested in a Building Society account in joint names actually belongs to husband and wife in unequal shares they can be taxed on their respective shares of the income. The married couple must then declare to the Inland Revenue how the account or other property and the income are shared between them. There is a special form to complete. The declaration applies from the date it is made.

Where one spouse transfers an income-producing asset to the other spouse knowing or expecting that the income will be credited to a joint account on which the donor spouse is free to draw, the income will still be regarded as belonging to the donor spouse for tax purposes.

9

THE FAMILY UNIT

Until the new system of Independent Taxation was introduced some four years ago, our tax system was built round the concept of the family unit. This is no longer so. Now, husbands and wives are taxed separately on their income and capital gains. They must complete their own Tax Returns each year and are responsible for settling their tax liabilities.

Marriage
Husband and wife are each entitled to personal allowances which can be set against their own income each year, whether this be from earnings or from investments. They can each have taxable income, after allowances and reliefs, of £23,700 for 1993/94 before either of them is liable to tax at the higher 40% rate. They may, of course, need to make some re-arrangements to their affairs if they are to take full advantage of opportunities to save tax under Independent Taxation.

Children
Children are also treated as separate individuals for tax purposes. The Income Tax liability of a minor child is calculated in exactly the same way as that for anyone else. A child is entitled to the personal allowance. If a son is married, he can claim the married couple's allowance.

If all this tempts you to think about giving some of your savings to your children so that the Income Tax on the interest or dividends can be recovered by set-off against their personal allowances, then I must warn you to proceed with caution. The income from a gift by a parent in favour of an unmarried minor/child is still regarded as the parent's income for tax purposes if it is paid out or applied for the child's benefit. If the income is accumulated, it will be treated as belonging to the child. Neither income nor capital should be used until the child is 18.

One way of using some of a child's personal allowance is by taking full advantage of the tax-free investment income a child can receive on capital from his or her parents. This annual limit is currently £100. This means that a married couple with two children can give away capital which will generate up to £400 in income per annum. Separate accounts should be opened for each child for the gifts from each parent. If, for some reason, the £100 limit is surpassed, the whole income — not just the excess over £100 — becomes taxable. Grandparents or other relatives can, however, give savings to their grandchildren or nieces, nephews, etc., without the same restrictions.

Most parents opt for either a building society or bank deposit account when investing their child's savings. In the previous chapter on investment income (Chapter 8), I mentioned that interest on, for example, a National Savings Bank investment account is not taxed at source, unlike that on a bank or building society account where the interest is paid to the investor after deduction of tax at the basic rate. Savers who are not taxpayers can receive gross interest on their bank or building society investments. This will be of considerable benefit to children. I referred to these arrangements in more detail in the previous chapter.

As an alternative to a Bank or Building Society account for your child's savings, why not take a look at the Children's Bonus Bonds issued by the Department for National Savings. They are particularly suitable for gifts from parents. The return on these bonds is exempt from both Income Tax and Capital Gains Tax. This tax exemption means that no parent can be liable to Income Tax on interest arising on the gift.

There is no general tax allowance for children. Child benefit, which is not taxable, is generally payable to the mother. The present rate is £10.20 per week for the first child and £8.25 for each subsequent child. There is an additional benefit of £6.15 each week for a single parent. You will probably be able to claim the additional personal allowance if you are single and have a child living with you (Chapter 2).

Responsibility for completing a minor's Income Tax Repayment Claim rests with the child's trustee or guardian. A minor/child is also a taxable person for the purposes of Capital Gains Tax (Chapter 11) and Inheritance Tax (Chapter 15).

Separation and divorce

Not only can the breakdown of a marriage cause much personal suffering, particularly when there are children of the marriage, but invariably it also calls for a reorganization of the parted couple's financial affairs. The full married couple's allowance is due in the year of separation.

I referred in Chapter 2 to the additional personal allowance and the situations when it can be claimed. When a couple split up any children of the marriage usually go and live with their mother. She can claim the additional personal allowance. Nevertheless, where a couple have at least two children it may be possible for both their father and mother to benefit from the additional personal allowance. Each would claim for one of the children.

Special rules apply to the tax treatment of maintenance payments under arrangements made before 15 March 1988 and court orders which had been applied for by then and were actually made before the end of June 1988. All maintenance payments under separation agreements or court orders must be made without deduction of Income Tax at the basic rate. They are deductible from the husband's income in calculating the tax he pays. In the hands of the recipient they are taxable income from which no tax has been deducted. The maximum amount eligible for tax relief is the amount on which relief was given for the year to 5 April 1989. This is also the same amount on which the recipient will be taxable.

As an alternative, you can elect to switch over to the new rules. These apply to court orders and maintenance agreements made on or after 15 March 1988. The divorced or separated husband will only qualify for tax relief where the payments are made to his former or separated wife. The maximum amount on which he is entitled to tax relief in any year is the difference between the married and single allowances; currently this is £1,720. No tax must be deducted at source from such payments. They do not count as taxable income in the hands of the recipient.

The Child Support Agency has taken over much of the work of the Courts on child maintenance. Maintenance assessed by the Agency qualifies for tax relief in the same way as maintenance under a court order. Furthermore, maintenance collected by the Agency on behalf of the divorced or separated spouse of the pair qualifies for tax relief in the same way as if the maintenance had been paid direct to the spouse.

Old age

Unfortunately, the elderly taxpayer has to cope with the tax system in exactly the same way as everyone else. Nevertheless, there are some factors which are only relevant in calculating the tax payable on the elderly person's income. First and foremost are the age allowances. In Chapter 2 I explained how a pensioner calculates whether he or she is entitled to these allowances.

Apart from the war widow's pension, a pension from either the State or a past employer's pension fund is taxable. Although it is taxable, no tax is deducted at source from the National Insurance Pension. A pension from a former employer's pension scheme is taxed under PAYE. In addition to including the pensioner's personal allowances the coding notice will incorporate a deduction equivalent to the State Retirement Pension. In this way the tax due on it is collected. The necessity of a direct payment of tax is avoided.

A code number ending with 'V' indicates the pensioner is entitled to the married couple's age allowance for age 65–74. A coding which includes the personal age allowance for 65–74 finishes up with 'P'. If you are entitled to the higher age allowances for age 75 or over, your coding will end with the letter T. The same applies where you do not receive the full age allowances because your income is over £14,200. In the exceptional situation of the deduction for the State Retirement Pension exceeding the pensioner's personal allowances, the Inland Revenue now issue a 'K' coding. The amount of the negative allowance is then added to your pension on which tax is to be paid. Nevertheless, there will still be some circumstances where it is just not possible to collect all the tax due on pensions under PAYE. Then it is necessary for the tax office to issue an assessment. The tax payable will be due in four equal instalments.

When a person starts to draw the old age pension, the Department of Social Security sends out a form to find out the tax office which deals with the pensioner's Tax Return. This enables the Department to tell the tax office of the amount of the new pensioner's National Insurance Pension and subsequent increases. This makes sure the correct deduction for the State pension is always included in the pensioner's code number.

With careful planning an elderly married couple with modest incomes may well be able to generate significant savings in their tax bills as the following example demonstrates.

Illustration

An elderly married couple both in their late 60s whose joint income for 1993/94 amounted to £20,700, paid Income Tax of £2,958.75 for the year. This all related to the husband's income as follows:

		Husband £		Wife £
State Pensions		2,917		1,752
Occupational Pensions		6,583		648
Building Society Interest				
— Gross equivalent		5,000		—
Interest on British Government Stocks		3,000		800
		17,500		3,200
Less: Allowances				
Personal/Personal age	3,445		4,200	
Married couple's	1,720		—	
		5,165		4,200
Taxable Income		£12,335		£—
Income Tax Payable:				
£2,500 @ 20%		500.00		—
£9,835 @ 25%		2,458.75		—
		£2,958.75		£—

The husband's income is above the upper limit beyond which he is not due either the personal age or married couple's age allowances. Also the wife has insufficient income to benefit from her full personal age allowance.

Significant tax savings of £750 for 1993/94 could have been achieved by the couple if the husband had transferred capital to his wife as follows:

	Husband £	Wife £
State Pensions	2,917	1,752
Occupational Pensions	6,583	648
Building Society Interest		
— Gross equivalent	2,500	2,500
Interest on British Government Stocks	1,200	2,600
	13,200	7,500

Less: Allowances				
Personal age	4,200		4,200	
Married couple's age	2,465		–	
		6,665		4,200
Taxable Income		£6,535		£3,300
Income Tax Payable:				
£2,500 @ 20%		500.00		500.00
£4,035/£800 @ 25%		1,008.75		200.00
		£1,508.75		£700.00

Death

Sadly, death comes to all of us and has consequences for taxation. There is no reduction in either the married couple's or married couple's age allowance, as the case may be, in the year of death of either spouse.

If the husband dies first he is entitled to his full personal allowance in the year of death. If his income that year is such that he is unable to use up the full married couple's or married couple's age allowance then the balance can be transferred to his widow. A widow can claim the widow's bereavement allowance for both the tax year in which her husband dies and the following tax year as long as she has not remarried by the beginning of that year.

Where the wife dies before her husband she will be due the full personal or, if appropriate, personal age allowance in the year of death.

10

THE OVERSEAS ELEMENT

Apart from some special cases, the amount of tax you pay each year depends on whether you are resident in the United Kingdom (UK) and, to a lesser extent, on your domicile status. If you live permanently in the UK then, generally, all your income arising in this country will be liable to UK taxation. Overseas income is similarly taxable although special rules apply in taxing foreign income of individuals not domiciled in the UK.

Not only are the two concepts of domicile and residence of fundamental importance in determining the extent of an individual's liability to UK taxation on income, they are of equal significance for the purposes of both Capital Gains Tax and Inheritance Tax.

Domicile
Your domicile will generally be considered to be the country or state which you regard as your permanent homeland. Your domicile is separate from your residence or nationality. When you are born you acquire a domicile of origin from your father. You can abandon your original domicile by birth if you settle in another country or state with a view to making it your new permanent home. Providing you sever all links with your current country of domicile you can move towards acquiring a domicile of choice in the new country. You should be prepared to provide a substantial amount of evidence that you propose to live there for ever.

A wife's domicile is not dependent on that of her husband if they were married at some time after the end of 1973. Prior to that time a woman automatically acquired the domicile of her husband on marriage.

If you think you have good grounds for believing that you should not be regarded as domiciled in the UK you should write to your tax office about this. Usually, you can then expect to receive a questionnaire which you should fill in and send back to your tax office. The information you have supplied will be considered by the Inland Revenue Specialist

Department which deals with these matters. In due course you will receive a ruling on your domicile status.

Residence and Ordinary Residence

There is no statutory definition of residence and ordinary residence. Each case must be judged on the facts. What follows is a summary of the main factors which will be taken into account.

Without exception you will always be regarded as resident in the UK if you spend 183 days or more here in the tax year. Days of arrival in, and departure from, the UK are normally left out of account in working out the number of days spent here.

If you are here for less than 183 days you will still be treated as resident where you visit the UK regularly and after four tax years your visits during those years average 91 days or more in a tax year. From the fifth year you are treated as UK resident.

You are also regarded as ordinarily resident in the UK if you are resident here from year to year. It is possible to be resident, but not ordinarily resident. For example, you may normally live outside the UK but are in this country for at least 183 days in a tax year. Conversely you can occasionally be considered to be ordinarily resident, not but actually resident, for a particular tax year. This could happen if you live in the UK but, for some reason, are abroad for a complete tax year.

Working Abroad – long absences

Poor job prospects in the UK, together with higher salaries and low taxation abroad may prompt you to look for work overseas. This is likely to involve living abroad permanently for a time. Your likely residence status is clearly set out in paragraphs 2:2 and 2:3 of the Inland Revenue booklet IR20 – *Residents and Non-Residents* – as follows:

> If you leave the UK to work full time abroad under a contract of employment, you are treated as not resident and not ordinarily resident if you meet all the following conditions:
>
> * Your absence from the UK and your employment abroad both last for at least a whole tax year.
> * During your absence any visits you make to the UK
>   – total less than 183 days in any tax year, and

- average less than 91 days a tax year (the average is taken over the period of absence up to a maximum of four years; any dates spent in the UK because of exceptional circumstances beyond your control, for example the illness of yourself or a member of your immediate family, are not normally counted for this purpose).

* For tax years before 1993/94, where there was accommodation in the UK available for your use, either all duties of your employment were performed abroad, or any duties you performed in the UK were incidental to your duties abroad.

If you meet all of the above conditions you are treated as not resident and not ordinarily resident in the UK from the day after you leave the UK to the date before you return to the UK at the end of your employment abroad. You are treated as coming to the UK permanently on the day you return from your employment abroad and as resident and ordinarily resident from that date.

There will be no tax to pay here on your salary for the part of the tax year after you have left the UK.

You may well take your spouse with you. By concession he or she may also be regarded as neither resident nor ordinarily resident for the same period even if your spouse does not work abroad.

Working Abroad – shorter absences

Where your job takes you overseas for shorter periods of absence then your tax treatment in the UK is still worked out on a favourable basis. Providing you can establish a consecutive period of at least 365 days working overseas, the exemption from Income Tax on the earnings from that employment is 100%. You are allowed intermittent visits to the UK in establishing a qualifying period of at least 365 days. These must not amount to 62 days, nor in building up the qualifying period must they come to more than one-sixth of the period starting from the outset.

Illustration
A businessman leaves the UK and is away for 102 days. He returns for 15 days before leaving for a further spell of 80 days. He then holidays in the UK for 14 days before a final period abroad of 160 days. All the periods can be linked up to make one qualifying period of 371 days.

Tax relief is allowed on travel expenses you incur in relation to your overseas employment. Nor will you be taxed on the cost of board and lodging provided for you where the expenses are borne by your employer.

Generally, whenever your job takes you overseas, even for short periods, you will not be taxed on the cost of your travelling expenses so long as your employer meets the bills. This also applies to the costs of unlimited return visits to the UK during longer assignments abroad.

No taxable benefit arises where your employer meets the travelling costs of your wife and children to visit you overseas. Not more than two return visits by the same person are allowed each year, and you must be working abroad for a continuous period of at least 60 days.

Leaving the UK permanently
Where you go abroad to live permanently you will provisionally be considered neither resident nor ordinarily resident in the UK from the day following your departure. You should be prepared to provide sufficient evidence of your intention to make a permanent home somewhere outside the UK. Providing you do not infringe the rules about visits to the UK the provisional non-resident ruling will subsequently be confirmed by the Inland Revenue. You are entitled to full allowances and reliefs for the year of departure.

When you become not ordinarily resident in the UK you can apply to receive interest on any bank or building society account here without deduction of tax. Similarly, Income Tax is not charged on the interest from certain UK Government Securities.

Allowances for non-UK residents
You may be able to claim UK tax allowances if you are not resident here. If you are eligible to claim you will generally be entitled to the same allowances as an individual resident in the UK. The following individuals can claim:

(1) A citizen of the Commonwealth, including Great Britain, or the Republic of Ireland.
(2) A present or former employee of the British Crown including his or her widow or widower.

(3) A resident of the Isle of Man or the Channel Islands.
(4) Certain other specific classes of individuals.

Many individuals choose to rent out their homes while they are away, particularly when they go to work abroad. The income from the letting will be taxable in the UK. However, they may be in a position to claim UK personal allowances to set against the rents less expenses.

Double taxation relief

If you move to a country with which the UK has concluded a Double Tax Agreement, you may be able to claim partial or full exemption from UK tax on certain types of income from UK sources. Normally, you should be entitled to some measure of relief from UK tax on pensions and annuities, royalties and dividends. Many Double Taxation Agreements contain clauses dealing with the special circumstances of teachers and researchers, students and apprentices, and entertainers and sportsmen/women.

Taking up UK residence

Perhaps you have been working overseas, your contract has come to an end and you are thinking about returning here. Before you take up UK residence again there are some specific tax-planning points which must be considered. For example, any bank deposit or building society accounts should be closed before you return as you could otherwise face the prospect of a charge to UK Income Tax on interest accrued, but not credited, during your period of non-residence.

If the UK is not your normal homeland you should initially be able to satisfy our Inland Revenue Authorities that you have an overseas domicile. Any income from investments here is taxable as it arises. Your overseas investment income is not taxed unless it is actually remitted or enjoyed here. Where your job is with either a UK or an overseas employer, and the duties of your employment are performed wholly in the UK, the full amount of your salary is taxable here.

You will be treated as resident and ordinarily resident from the date you arrive if you are either coming here permanently or intending to stay for at least three years. You will be able to claim full UK personal allowances for the year of arrival.

11

CAPITAL GAINS TAX

As its name implies, Capital Gains Tax is a tax on profits you realize from the disposal of capital assets. As with most other forms of taxation there is the usual list of exceptions to this general rule. Gambling or pools winnings and personal or professional damages are not taxable. Neither are gains realized on disposing of any of the assets in the following table:

> Private cars
> National Savings
> Your private residence
> Chattels, with an expected life of more than 50 years, sold for less than £6,000
> British government securities and corporate bonds
> Shares issued under the Business Expansion Scheme after 18 March 1986 on their first disposal. For the exemption to apply, the Income Tax relief granted must not have been withdrawn.
> Shares issued under the Enterprise Investment Scheme on their first disposal, so long as the tax relief has not been withdrawn.
> Investments in a Personal Equity Plan
> Life assurance policies
> Charitable gifts
> Gifts for the public benefit
> Foreign currency for personal expenditure

The list of taxable gains includes profits made from disposing of property, shareholdings, unit trust holdings, works of art and foreign currency for other than personal expenditure.

Rate of tax

For the 1993/94 tax year the first £5,800 of chargeable gains you realize are tax free. The annual exemption limit applies to both husband and wife. Gains in excess of the annual tax-free allowance are charged at your Income Tax rates found by adding the gains to your taxable income.

Illustration

A taxpayer realized gains of £14,500 during 1993/94. His taxable income, after personal allowances and reliefs, was £17,000. The Capital Gains Tax he owes for the year is £2,475 as follows:

	£
Realized gains	14,500
Less: Exemption limit	5,800
	£8,700
Tax payable:	
£6,700 at 25%	1,675
£2,000 at 40%	800
1993/94 Capital Gains Tax payable	£2,475

The amount of Capital Gains Tax at 25% is worked out on the difference between the £23,700 limit of income taxable at the lower and basic rates and the taxpayer's income of £17,000.

Any allowances or reliefs which you are unable to use because your income is too low cannot be set against your capital gains.

Husband and wife

Under Independent Taxation husband and wife are taxed separately on the chargeable gains they realize in a tax year above the annual exemption limit. A married couple living together can transfer assets between them free of tax. The indexation allowance is due up to the date of the transfer. The calculation of the indexation allowance for the transferee on the eventual disposal of the asset is more complicated. This exemption from tax ceases to apply when a couple permanently separate.

In cases where a married couple hold an asset in their joint names, any gain is apportioned between them in the ratio of their respective interests in the asset at the time of disposal. This treatment may not necessarily follow the split of the income for income tax purposes. Here the law generally assumes a married couple are equally entitled to the income even if in fact, this is not so. Where a couple have jointly made a declaration to the Inland Revenue of the ratio in which an asset and the income derived from it are shared between them, the same split will be followed for Capital Gains Tax purposes.

Losses

Losses can be set against gains made in the same tax year. Unused losses can be carried forward to be set against gains in subsequent tax years without time limit. They then reduce the amount of your gains in excess of the annual exemption limit.

Illustration

A taxpayer had capital losses of £6,400 available for carry-forward at 5 April 1993. During 1993/94 the taxpayer realized gains of £9,500 and made losses of £1,300.

The capital gains position for the year is:

	£	£
Gains realized in the year		9,500
Less: Losses: in the year	1,300	
brought forward (part)	2,400	
		3,700
1993/94 Exemption limit		£5,800

The unused losses of £4,000 can be carried forward to be set against gains in later years.

Losses realized by one spouse cannot be set against gains realized by the other spouse. This restriction on the set-off of losses also extends to unused losses at 5 April 1990. This was the last date before the introduction of Independent Taxation.

A loss arising on the sale or gift of an investment to a person connected with the individual making the disposal can only be set off against a gain from a similar disposal at a later date.

Where the value of an asset becomes negligible or nil, the loss can be claimed without actually disposing of the asset. In these hard-pressed times, and with ever increasing numbers of company failures, this form of loss relief should not be overlooked. The loss arises on the date that the relief is claimed. In practice, however, a two-year period is allowed from the time the asset became of negligible value.

Another form of loss relief applies if you have subscribed for shares in a trading company not quoted on a recognized Stock Exchange. Where you make a loss on disposing of such shares, or they become worthless, the loss can be set against your income rather than against other capital gains. The claim for this sort of treatment must be made within two years after the end of the tax year in which the relief is taken.

The computation of gains

The taxable gain on the disposal of an asset is calculated by making various deductions from the price realized on sale, as follows:

(1) The cost of acquisition, and
(2) The incidental costs of buying and selling the asset, and
(3) Any additional expenditure incurred on enhancing the value of the asset during the period of ownership, and
(4) The indexation allowance.

There are occasions when a different figure from the actual disposal proceeds is substituted in the calculation. For example, this happens when you make a gift or sell an asset at a nominal value to a close member of your family. You must then bring into the computation of the capital gain the open-market value of the asset at the time of disposal.

The date of sale of an asset is taken as the date when the contract for sale is made. The same rule applies to the date of acquisition.

Later on in this chapter I shall deal with the special rules in cases where you dispose of assets you owned on either 6 April 1965 or 31 March 1982.

The indexation allowance

This allowance measures the impact of inflation on both the cost of an asset and any other expenditure you have incurred on enhancing its value. The rules dealing with the calculation of the allowance are:

(1) The allowance is governed by the movement in the Retail Prices Index in the period of ownership. For assets which you have owned since before April 1982 the starting date for calculating the indexation allowance is March 1982.

(2) When you dispose of an asset which you acquired before 6 April 1982 the indexation allowance can be calculated on either the market value of the asset at

31 March 1982 or its actual cost, whichever is greater. Where you elect for the capital gains on all disposals of assets which you owned on 31 March 1982 to be worked out on their values at that date, ignoring original costs, the indexation allowance can only be calculated on those values.

(3) The allowance will not be given where an asset is sold at a loss. Neither can the indexation allowance turn a gain into a loss. It can only serve to reduce a gain to nil. This change in the rules applies to disposals on or after 30 November 1993. Up until then the indexation allowance was available on losses and to turn gains into losses.

Table 5 at the end of the book sets out the indexation allowance for assets disposed of between April and December 1993.

Illustration

A freehold property was purchased in November 1985 for £40,000. The legal fees and stamp duty on the purchase came to £1,340. An extension was added in February 1988 at a cost of £9,400.

Contracts for sale were exchanged in September 1993. It was sold for £88,000. The estate agents' commission, including the costs of advertising, and solicitors' fees came to £2,585.

The indexation allowance between November 1985 and September 1993 is 0.479, and from February 1988 to September 1993 is 0.368.

The chargeable gain is £11,414 as follows:

	£	£
Sale price		88,000
Less: Costs of sale		2,585
		85,415
Less: Acquisition price	40,000	
Costs of purchase	1,340	
Enhancement expenditure — extension	9,400	
	50,740	
Indexation allowance:		
£41,340 × 0.479	19,802	
£9,400 × 0.368	3,459	
		74,001
Chargeable gain		£11,414

Assets owned on 31 March 1982

Gains and losses on disposals of assets which you owned on 31 March 1982 can be calculated solely by reference to their market value at that date, ignoring original costs. In most cases, these rules will mean your capital gains are reduced compared with the calculation based on historical cost only.

Illustration

A freehold property purchased in 1976 for £20,000 was sold in May 1993 for £84,000. At 31 March 1982 it was valued at £39,000. The indexation allowance between March 1982 and May 1993 is 0.776.

The chargeable gain is £14,736 as follows:

	£	On 31 March 1982 Value £	£	On Historical Cost £
Sale price		84,000		84,000
Less: March 1982 value	39,000		–	
Acquisition cost	–		20,000	
Indexation allowance £39,000 × 0.776	30,264	69,264	30,264	50,264
		£14,736		£33,736
1993/94 Chargeable gain		£14,736		

Needless to say, there are special rules where the calculations based firstly on the March 1982 value and secondly on historical cost give different results, as follows:

On March 1982 Value	On Historical Cost	Chargeable Gain/Loss
Gain of £3,810	Gain of £2,150	£2,150 Gain
Loss of £515	Loss of £95	£95 Loss
Loss of £490	Gain of £760	neither gain nor loss
Gain of £2,435	Loss of £1,640	neither gain nor loss

You can, however, elect for the capital gains on all disposals of assets which you owned on 31 March 1982 to be worked out by reference to their values at that date, ignoring original costs. Once made, the election cannot be revoked. It can be made at any time within two years after the end of the tax year in which the first disposal of an asset you owned on 31 March 1982 takes place.

Quoted stocks and shares

Prior to 6 April 1982 each shareholding was regarded as a single asset. This was commonly known as a 'pool'. Each additional purchase of the same class of shares or a sale of part of the holding represented either an addition to, or a disposal out of, the pool. With the introduction of the indexation allowance this changed. Each shareholding acquired after 5 April 1982 represented a separate asset. A subsequent addition to a holding you owned at 5 April 1982 could not be added to the pool.

As from 6 April 1985 the rules were altered once more. Shares of the same class are again regarded as a single asset growing or diminishing on each acquisition or disposal. This form of 'pooling' applies to shares acquired after 5 April 1982 unless they had already been disposed of before 6 April 1985; it is called a 'new holding'. A pool which was frozen under the 1982 rules stays that way. It remains a single asset which cannot grow by subsequent acquisitions and is known as a '1982 holding'. The rules are even more complicated where you may still own any shares which were acquired before 6 April 1965. A '1982 holding' is treated like any other asset in calculating the indexation allowance. This is not so for a 'new holding'. It is to be kept continually indexed each time there is either an addition to or a disposal out of the pool.

The procedure for matching shares sold with their corresponding acquisition is as follows:

(1) Shares acquired on the same day.

(2) Shares acquired in the nine days preceding a disposal on a first-in first-out basis.

(3) Shares comprised in a 'new holding'.

(4) Shares within a '1982 holding'.

Illustration

A taxpayer made the following purchases in the shares of a quoted company:

Date	Number of Shares	Cost
May 1974	1,500	£1,875
Jan 1981	2,500	£3,500
Mar 1985	3,000	£3,900
Feb 1988	2,000	£3,500

In July 1993 he sold 8,000 shares for £22,400. The shares were valued at £1.50 each on 31 March 1982. The indexation allowance is:

0.771 between March 1982 and July 1993
0.117 between March 1985 and February 1988
0.357 between February 1988 and July 1993

5,000 shares sold must first of all be identified with those in the 'new holding' as follows:

	£
Cost of 3,000 shares in March 1985	3,900
Indexation allowance to February 1988 – 0.117	456
	4,356
Cost of 2,000 shares in February 1988	3,500
	7,856
Indexation allowance to July 1993 – 0.357	2,804
	10,660
Proceeds of sale of 5,000 shares	14,000
Chargeable gain	£3,340

The remaining 3,000 shares sold are then identified with part of the shares acquired before 31 March 1982. As the average cost is £1.34 per share it is beneficial to base the capital gain on the share price at 31 March 1982 as follows:

	£
Value of 3,000 shares at March 1982	4,500
Indexation allowance to July 1993 – 0.771	3,469
	7,969
Proceeds of sale of 3,000 shares	8,400
Chargeable gain	£431

The total chargeable gain on the sale is £3,771

Whenever you receive a bonus issue of shares of the same class as an existing holding the date of their acquisition is the same as that of the original holding.

If you take up a rights issue to subscribe for additional shares in a company where you are already a shareholder, the indexation allowance on the cost price of the extra shares runs from the date they are acquired, not from the date when the original holding was bought.

Where a company in which you have a holding is taken over, and instead of receiving cash you exchange your shares for shares in the new company, no disposal takes place at that time. Your new holding is regarded as having been acquired at the same time and for the same price as the old one.

One of the consequences of the changes in procedure for matching shares is that the well-known practice of establishing losses by 'bed-and-breakfasting' shares is possible under the simple procedure of sale and repurchase on consecutive days within the same Stock Exchange account.

Unquoted Investments

Many of the rules dealing with quoted stocks and shares also apply to computations on disposals of unquoted investments. For example, the indexing rules apply in the same way as they do to quoted shares.

Most of the special rules dealing with unquoted investments apply to assets held at 6 April 1965 when Capital Gains Tax was introduced.

Assets held on 6 April 1965

Following the introduction of rules dealing with assets owned on 31 March 1982, the special rules for assets held on 6 April 1965 are likely to be of less significance. The method of computation is known as 'time-apportionment'. It does not apply to quoted stocks and shares, only to unquoted investments and other assets such as land. Time-apportionment is designed to eliminate from the charge to tax the profit on sale attributable to the period up to 5 April 1965. This result is achieved by assuming that the asset increased in value at a standard rate throughout the period of ownership. It is the gain, net of indexation, that is time-apportioned. For assets other than quoted stocks and shares, acquired before 6 April 1945, the time-apportionment benefit is limited to 20 years.

Instead of relying on the time-apportionment method, a taxpayer can elect for the value of the asset on 6 April 1965 to be substituted in a calculation of the capital gain arising on sale. The election is irrevocable and must be made within two years of the end of the tax year in which the disposal is made.

Illustration

A property purchased in June 1959 for £2,500 was sold in August 1993 for £43,000. An election for the 6 April 1965 value is not beneficial. At 31 March 1982 it was worth £20,000. The indexation allowance between March 1982 and August 1993 is 0.779.

The first calculation of the chargeable gain is:

	£
Sale proceeds	43,000
Less: Purchase price	2,500
Gross gain	£40,500

Time-apportionment:

$$\frac{\text{April 1965 to August 1993} = 340 \text{ months}}{\text{June 1959 to August 1993} = 410 \text{ months}} \times £40,500 = £33,585$$

Less: Indexation allowance £20,000 × 0.779	15,580
Chargeable gain	£18,005

The second calculation of the chargeable gain is:

	£	£
Sale proceeds		43,000
Less: 31 March 1982 value	20,000	
Indexation allowance £20,000 × 0.779	15,580	35,580
Chargeable gain		£ 7,420

It is to the taxpayer's advantage for the 31 March 1982 value to be used in calculating the capital gain.

A taxpayer can elect for the capital gains or losses on disposals of quoted shares and securities held at 6 April 1965 to be calculated by substituting the 6 April 1965 values for the original costs in all cases. Separate elections must be made for the taxpayer and spouse and they are required both for ordinary shares and for fixed interest securities. The election for each category is irrevocable. It has to be made within two years of the end of the tax year in which the first sale after 19 March 1968 occurs. If no election is made the capital gain is worked out by comparing the disposal proceeds with the original cost and value of the holding on 6 April 1965.

Where, as is more likely, a taxpayer has elected for the capital gains on disposals of all assets owned on 31 March 1982 to be worked out solely by reference to their values at that date, the above rules setting out the alternatives available for assets held on 6 April 1965 will be superseded.

Your private residence

The profit on a sale of your home is exempt from tax. The exemption extends to the house and its garden or grounds up to half a hectare, including the land on which the house is built. A larger area can qualify for exemption where it can be shown that it was needed to enjoy the house. Where a home has not been occupied as your private residence throughout the full period of ownership, or, if later, since 31 March 1982, a proportion of the gain on sale becomes taxable. Nevertheless, certain periods of absence are disregarded in determining whether the gain is totally exempt from tax. These are the last three years of ownership in any event and generally those when you have to live away from home because of your work.

Illustration

A taxpayer realized a capital gain of £68,000 when he sold his home in December 1993. It had been acquired back in May 1984. He was employed abroad between October 1984 and February 1986. In March 1990 he moved out into his new home.

Both the time spent working overseas and the last three years are regarded as periods when the home was the taxpayer's main residence. The chargeable period is, therefore, only nine months and the chargeable gain is £5,321 as follows:

$$\frac{\text{Chargeable period}}{\text{Period of ownership}} = \frac{9 \text{ months}}{115 \text{ months}} \times £68,000 = £5,321$$

Where part of your home is used exclusively for business purposes the proportion of the profit on sale attributable to the business use is a chargeable gain. Whether part of your home is actually used exclusively for business use is entirely a matter of fact. If you let part of your home as residential accommodation, the gain on the part which has been let is either wholly or partly exempt from tax. The proportion of the profit on sale which is exempt is the lower of either £40,000 or an amount equivalent to the gain on the part you have occupied as your home. The same applies when you let out your entire home.

Illustration

A taxpayer made a capital gain of £94,000 when he disposed of his home in November 1993. It had been bought in June 1987. The taxpayer and his family lived there until October 1987 and from October 1990 up to the date of sale. In the intervening period it was let. This period of absence was not one when the home was still regarded as the taxpayer's main residence.

The chargeable gain is only £3,949 as follows:

	£	£
Capital gain (period of ownership – 77 months)		94,000
Less: Main residence exemption – 41 months	50,051	
Letting exemption – 36 months (lower of £40,000 or £50,051)	40,000	
		90,051
Chargeable gain		£ 3,949

Alternatively, if you take in lodgers who mix in and eat with your family, the Inland Revenue take the view that no part of the exemption on a sale of your home is lost. Nor should any capital gain arise if you take advantage of the rent-a-room scheme mentioned in Chapter 8.

A second home

If you have two homes such as a house or flat in town for use during the weekdays and a cottage in the country for weekends, the profit on sale of only one of them is exempt from tax. Which one counts as your main residence is a matter of fact. It is, however, possible for you to determine this by writing to your tax office. In the election you should request which of your homes you want regarded as your principal private residence for Capital Gains Tax purposes. The election should apply from the date when you first have at least two homes available to you. It can be made at any time in the two years beginning with the date from which it is to apply. You are, of course, free to vary it as and when it suits you. If you own a home which was occupied rent free by the same dependent relative both on 5 April 1988 and throughout your period of ownership, then the profit on sale is tax free. Otherwise, it is likely that part of the gain will be taxable.

Chattels

Gains on the sales of chattels with an expected life of more than 50 years sold for less than £6,000 are exempt from tax. For items which fetch between £6,000 and £15,000 the chargeable gain is restricted to 5/3 times the amount of the proceeds of sale (ignoring expenses) over £6,000 where this is to the taxpayer's advantage.

Illustration

A piece of antique furniture purchased in 1985 for £1,500 was sold in August 1993 for £9,000. Although the profit on sale was £7,500 the chargeable gain, ignoring the indexation allowance, is restricted to £5,000, being 5/3 × (£9,000−£6,000).

Where an article is sold at a loss for under £6,000, the allowable loss is restricted by assuming the proceeds on sale were equivalent to £6,000.

Illustration

A painting was purchased many years ago for £10,670. It subsequently transpired that it was a fake and was sold for £410. The loss on sale, ignoring the indexation allowance, is restricted to £4,670, being £10,670 less £6,000.

Articles comprising a set are regarded as a single item when they are sold to the same person but at different times.

Wasting assets

Wasting assets are assets with an expected life span of less than 50 years. Unless it comes within the definition of 'tangible moveable property' a gain on the sale of a wasting asset is calculated in the same way as that on the sale of any other asset, except that the purchase price wastes away during the asset's expected life span. Leases of land for less than 50 years are wasting assets. A specific table is provided for calculating the proportion of the purchase price of a lease which can be deducted from the sale proceeds.

The gain on a sale of a wasting asset which is also 'tangible moveable property' is exempt from tax. Neither does a loss on a sale of similar property count as an allowable loss.

Part disposals

Where you only sell part of an asset its acquisition cost is apportioned between the part sold and the proportion retained. This is done on a pro rata basis by reference to the proceeds of sale of the part sold and the open-market value of the proportion retained. The indexation allowance is calculated on the cost of the part sold. The proportion of the original cost of the asset attributable to the part which was not sold can be set against the proceeds on a sale of the remainder at a later date. This calculation must be reworked on the 31 March 1982 value of an asset acquired before that date where the part disposal took place before 6 April 1988.

If the part sold is small compared with the value of the entire asset or shareholding you can claim to deduct the sale proceeds from the acquisition cost. Where the part disposal is one of land this procedure can be adopted so long as the sale proceeds are both less than £20,000 and one fifth of the value of the remaining land.

Business assets

If you are in business and dispose of an asset used in your trade you have to pay Capital Gains Tax on the profit of sale. The profit or loss is calculated in the same way as that on a disposal of an asset you own personally. If the proceeds of sale are reinvested wholly or partly in other assets for use in the business, payment of the tax on the profit can be wholly or partly postponed by reducing the cost of the replacement assets by the capital gain realized on the disposal of the old asset.

When you come to dispose of your business assets on retirement either by sale or gift the first £250,000 (£150,000 up to 30 November 1993) and 50% of the next £750,000 (£450,000 up to 30 November 1993) of capital gains are exempt from tax. To qualify automatically for this maximum exemption you must have been in business for at least 10 years and be over age 55 at the time of the disposal. The same age qualification applies to both sexes. You can only claim this relief before age 55 if you retire prematurely owing to ill health.

The precise rules which apply in calculating the capital gain on the disposal of a business asset during the course of trading or on retirement are complicated. It is outside the scope of this book to go into them in detail. The indexation allowance features in both of them.

Re-investment relief

A new Capital Gains Tax relief for entrepreneurs selling their own company and re-investing in an unquoted trading company was introduced in March 1993. This allowed entrepreneurs to defer any chargeable gain on the sale of their company provided various conditions were met. This re-investment relief is extended for disposals on or after 30 November 1993. All chargeable gains now realized by individuals can be deferred if they are re-invested in eligible shares in unquoted trading companies.

To qualify for this relief the chargeable gains must be re-invested within a period beginning one year before, and ending three years after, the original disposal. There is no requirement on the investor to take a minimum holding in the unquoted trading company. Tax on the original gain will remain deferred while the new shares are held. If, however, the unquoted trading company ceases to meet the qualifying conditions at any time within three years after the re-investment is made, or if the shareholder emigrates within this three year period, then the deferred gain will be brought into charge to tax.

As with the previous section on business assets, the legislation dealing with this re-investment relief is lengthy. It contains a number of conditions and restrictions and is an area where you will inevitably need to seek professional advice.

Gifts

The capital gain on a gift is calculated by using the market value of the asset at the date of gift. The amount of the gain is reduced by the indexation allowance which is due at the time.

Where the gift is one of business assets you can elect with the transferee for payment of the tax on the gift to be postponed until the asset is subsequently disposed of by the transferee. This same rule also applies in other restricted circumstances. For gifts of some assets where deferral is not available the Capital Gains Tax can be paid in 10 equal annual instalments.

Deferred gains on business assets and gifts

Earlier in this chapter you read about the rules for working out the capital gains on assets which you owned at the end of March 1982. In the preceding two sections I made mention of postponing the payment of Capital Gains Tax on gifts and the proceeds of sale of business assets which are reinvested in other assets for use in the business.

Without some special form of relief, the benefit of these rules would be denied where a deferral occurred in the period from 31 March 1982 to 5 April 1988, and a charge to Capital Gains Taxes arises thereafter since the disposal is not of an asset owned on 31 March 1982. The remedy provides for a 50% reduction of the deferred gain.

Illustration

A business asset purchased in 1978 was sold in January 1986. The deferred gain on the sale was £56,000. The replacement asset cost £120,000 and was sold in May 1993 for £180,000. The indexation allowance between January 1986 and May 1993 is 0.466. The chargeable gain is £41,128 as follows:

	£	£
Sale proceeds		180,000
Less: Purchase price	120,000	
Less: Deferred gain	56,000	
	64,000	
Add: 50% of postponed gain	28,000	
	92,000	
Indexation allowance		
£92,000 × 0.466	42,872	138,872
1993/94 Chargeable gain		£41,128

The relief must be claimed within two years of the end of the year of assessment in which the disposal takes place.

Inheritances

No Capital Gains Tax is payable on the unrealized profits on your assets at the date of your death. When you inherit an asset you acquire it at the value on the date of death of the deceased. Generally, this rule is also applied whenever you become entitled to assets from a trust.

12

COMPLETING THE RETURN

When you collect your post up from the doormat you can always pick out your Tax Return from the other letters. It comes in a distinctive brown envelope at the same time every year. Try to avoid the temptation to put it to one side. Although it may not prove possible to complete the Return and send it back to your tax office within the required 30 days, it is better to deal with it promptly. At least your tax office can then see that you are being given the correct allowances and reliefs in the code number which your employer is using to calculate the regular deductions for PAYE from your salary or wages. If your Return shows that you owe some additional tax on your income or you have realized some capital gains, the Inspector of Taxes will send you any assessments to collect the tax due. Failure to deal with your Tax Return quickly can often result in the Inland Revenue sending you assessments showing your income has been estimated. What you do when you receive one of these is dealt with in Chapter 13. Alternatively, you may render yourself liable to an interest charge. This is dealt with in the last section in this chapter.

Not everyone is sent a Tax Return. If you do not receive one it is probably because your tax office think your only income is your salary or wage taxed under PAYE. If this is so and you are satisfied you are being given all the personal allowances and reliefs which you claim you need do nothing more. On the other hand, if you have received additional income which is taxable you should ask for a Tax Return so you can declare it to the Inland Revenue and pay any tax due on it. Failure to do this will lead to the imposition of both interest and penalties.

With your Tax Return comes a guide called 'Filling in your 1994 Tax Return', which will help you complete the form correctly. You should also read the notes on the left hand side of each page of the Return. They include a reference to those Inland Revenue leaflets listed in Table 1 at the end of the book which are relevant to your particular circumstances.

There are several different types of Income Tax Return.

The following list shows which one you can expect to receive:

Form Number	Classification of Taxpayer
11	Standard full return for self-employed person
11P	Standard full return for employee
11K	Non-domiciled individual
11 (Lloyds)	Lloyds underwriter
P1	Simplified return for employee
R40	Taxpayer entitled to a repayment
R40(S)	Tax repayment claim for student
R232	Minors repayment claim

This book is being published at about the time you should be receiving your 1994 Tax Return. The form serves two purposes. It acts as a report of your income, outgoings and capital gains for the year ended on 5 April 1994, but the section on allowances is for the year to 5 April 1995.

As there is not a great deal of space in each section of the Return you can always provide more detailed information on a separate statement and only show the total income for a particular item on the form. When you do this every item on your Return for which there is a supporting statement should be noted 'see schedule attached' or words to that effect.

The Tax Return form has recently been completely re-written and enlarged. It now runs to 12 full A4 size pages. Unfortunately, owing to lack of space, it is not possible to reproduce the entire Return. I will concentrate on those sections which are likely to be relevant to the majority of taxpayers. When the Return is finished it must be signed in the space provided on the back page. Bear in mind the wording of the Declaration: 'The information I have given on this form is correct and complete to the best of my knowledge and belief.'

Income

If you are self-employed you will have to prepare a statement of the income and expenses from your business along the lines of the Profit and Loss account for David Smith's Art Gallery as set out in Chapter 6. Based on these accounts

104 COMPLETING THE RETURN

he would make the following entries in his Tax Return:

Notes
These notes give guidance and refer you to relevant parts in the leaflet 'Filling in your 1994 Tax Return

Income from self-employment - year to 5 April 1994

Complete this section if you have income from self-employment. If you are in partnership give details for your share in the partnership only.

See note 2 about keeping records. See note 3 about partnerships.

Details of your business
Business name, (and address if different from the address above)

> DAVID SMITH
> 40 BARN LANE
> FIELDGATE
> TA6 7 DZ

State what kind of self-employed work you do

> ART GALLERY PROPRIETOR

See note 4 and page 4 of this form.
See notes 5 and 6.

Tick here if providing furnished accommodation in your only or main home amounts to a trade and you are in the *Rent-a Room* scheme. ☐

Businesses with a turnover of less than £15,000

Ask for "Simple Tax Accounts" (leaflet IR104)

If you were in business on your own, or in partnership, and your turnover (or the partnership's turnover) was less than £15,000 a year you do not need to send accounts. You may, instead, give details of turnover and allowable business expenses.

Turnover £ _____   **Allowable business expenses** £ _____

See note 6 for expenses.
See note 7 for losses.
11 (1994)

All businesses: Profit for tax purposes
Your profit for tax purposes is your turnover less allowable business expenses. It does not include enterprise allowance received. Give your profit for the accounting period you specify below. If you have made a loss enter 'Nil'.   **£25,210**

Notes
See note 2.

Accounts
If your turnover was £15,000 or more, you should return this form with a statement of your profit or loss for tax purposes supported by full accounts. You should also do this if your turnover was less than £15,000 and you choose not to enter your turnover and expenses above.

Period covered by your accounts or statement of turnover and expenses
Give the period covered by your accounts (or the partnership accounts), or by the statement of turnover and expenses above, which ended on a date between 6 April 1993 and 5 April 1994. If you stopped being self-employed, give the date you stopped.

See note 8.   **Start of period**   01 / 08 / 1992   **End of period**   31 / 07 / 1993

See note 9.
Capital allowances
Give the amount you are claiming or tick here and give details on a separate sheet of paper if you want your Tax Office to help work out the figure.   **£ 2750**

See note 10.
Balancing adjustments
Give the amount of the adjustments or tick here and give details on a separate sheet of paper if you want your Tax Office to help work out the figure.   £ _____

See note 11.
Enterprise allowance received   £ _____

To find out if you qualify see note 12.
Further relief on Class 4 National Insurance
Type of relief _____   Amount. £ _____

Form P60 – Your certificate of pay and Tax Deducted – given to you by your employer shortly after the end of the tax year – will tell you the amount of your salary or wages to enter on the Tax Return. You should keep this form so that if you receive a formal assessment on your earnings you can check the figure of tax deducted from them with that shown on the P60. If you are a company director or earn more than £8,500 per annum your employer will complete a form P11D detailing your benefits-in-kind and other expenses payments. You should ask for a copy of this and enter your taxable benefits.

INCOME 105

Income from employment etc - year to 5 April 1994

See note 13.

Complete this section if you worked for any employer full-time, part-time or on a casual basis or for an agency. Also fill it in if you received director's fees or payments or benefits from any office you held.

If you have been given a form P60 by your employer, it should contain the information you need. Give your income before tax. If you are a director see note 14. If you are not a director see note 15.

Wages, salary, fees, bonuses etc.
Your occupation and employer's name(s) and address(es)

| DESIGNER   FIELDGATE TEXTILE Co LTD
FLOWERS LANE
FIELDGATE
TA6 5NZ | £ 22,000 |

Some of these are not liable to tax. See note 16.

Lump sum and compensation payments
Give the amount of any lump sum or compensation payment you received during 1993-94, if this has not already been included in *Wages, salary, fees, bonuses etc* above.

£

Profit-related pay and profit sharing schemes

Give the number of profit-related pay schemes to which you belong ☐

Tick here if you received a taxed sum from the trustees of an approved profit-sharing scheme. ☐

Tick here if this sum is included under *Wages, salary, fees, bonuses etc* above. ☐

Include cash-in-hand payments, casual earnings, tips and any other payments.

Other payments
Give the amount and the type of work you did and the name(s) and address(es) of any employer(s) (if as above, write 'As above').

£

Business mileage is mileage necessarily travelled in the course of your work. It does not usually include mileage between home and work. See note 17.

Cars and car fuel
Tick here if you or a member of your family or household were provided with a car during the year because of your job and it was available for private use. ✓

Tick the box corresponding with your business mileage in the car.

2,500 or less ☐   2,501 to 17,999 ✓   18,000 or over ☐

If you received car fuel for private travel in the car provided for you (or for a member of your family or household) tick the appropriate box.

petrol ✓   diesel ☐

Notes
For examples of the most common benefits see note 17.

Other benefits in kind and expenses allowances
List the benefits and give their values if you know them. List also types of expenses allowances made to you and give the total amounts. You can leave out altogether (in this item and in the next item) all amounts where the Inland Revenue has agreed with your employer that the expenses are allowable and no tax will be payable (a *dispensation*).

| MEDICAL INSURANCE | £ 400 |

See note 18.

Expenses for which you wish to claim a deduction
List here the types of expenses and give the amounts

| INSTITUTE OF DESIGNERS - SUBSCRIPTION | £ 30 |

The amount of your pension from a previous employer's pension fund will also be notified to you on a Form P60. If you are drawing the National Insurance Retirement Pension you should declare the amount of your income for the 52 week period to 5 April 1994. Particularly where your National Insurance Pension is paid quarterly, there will be a small

106 COMPLETING THE RETURN

difference between the income you should show on the Return and the actual pension received during the tax year. Pensioners are also asked for additional information about the amounts and frequency of payment of the various pensions they receive so that their tax office can ensure they pay the right amount of tax.

Income from Pensions and Superannuation – year to 5 April 1994

If you want more information ask for Income Tax and Pensioners (leaflet IR121). See note 20 for what counts as a pension.

Complete this section if you received or were entitled to a pension in 1993-94.

State Pensions
Give the full amount you were entitled to in 1993-94. If you are a married woman you should enter the pension payable to you, even if it was paid to you as a result of your husband's contributions. Include widow's pension here but include widowed mother's allowance under *Other Social Security benefits overleaf*.
If you are a married man enter only the amount payable to you.

£ 2,917

You should find the information you need on the form P60 which the payer should have given you after the end of the tax year, or any other certificate of pension paid and tax deducted. See note 19 if your pension is from abroad.

Other Pensions
Include:
- pensions from a former employer (paid either in the UK or abroad)
- pensions you receive from your late husband's/wife's former employer (paid either in the UK or abroad)
- pensions from a personal pension plan or retirement annuity contract
- pensions from Free Standing Additional Voluntary Contribution Schemes
- pensions for injuries at work or for work-related illness
- other pensions from abroad
- pensions from service in the armed forces.

Do **not** include war widows' pensions and pensions for wounds or disability in military service or for other war injuries as these are not taxable.

Give the name(s) and address(es) of the payer(s) of the pension and the full amount of your pension(s) for the 1993-94 tax year.

```
FIELDGATE PUBLISHING CO LTD
BUSH ROAD
FIELDGATE  TA6 3DY
```
£ 3600

Surpluses repaid from a Free Standing Additional Voluntary Contributions scheme
Complete this item if, when you retired or left pensionable service, some of your contributions from a free-standing additional voluntary contributions (FSAVC) scheme were repaid to you. **Give the gross amount shown on the certificate given to you by the scheme administrator.**

£

Notes

Income from pensions – year to 5 April 1995

This section asks for pension(s) information for the year ending on 5 April 1995. The pension section on the previous page asked you for details about your pension(s) for the year which ended on 5 April 1994.

If you currently receive a pension or expect to start receiving a pension before 6 April 1995, please give the details asked for below. In the column headed "Amount of pension you receive or expect to receive", please show:

- for pensions you already receive - the amount you get at the time you fill the form in
- for pensions you expect to start receiving - the amount you will get (if you know it).

See note 20 for what counts as a state pension

Starting date (if after 5 April 1994)	Amount of pension you receive or expect to receive	Say whether this is per week, every 4 weeks, each month, every 3 months or per year	Tick if this is after tax	Tick if a state pension
/ /19	£ 749	EVERY 3 MONTHS		✓
/ /19	£ 300	EVERY MONTH		
/ /19	£			
/ /19	£			
/ /19	£			
/ /19	£			

The next part of the Return form requires you to declare those National Insurance and Social Security benefits received in the tax year which are taxable. This applies to Unemployment Benefit or Income Support, or Widowed Mother's Allowance and other benefits. The taxable and non-taxable Social Security benefits are summarized in Table 8 at the end of the book. In general, benefits which replace earnings are taxable. Those intended to meet a specific need are not taxable.

Your managing agents will have regularly sent you statements showing the rents receivable and expenses incurred for any properties which you let out. From these you should prepare a summary to accompany your Tax Return along the lines of the example in Chapter 8. You should also tick the right box on the Tax Return to show the type of rental. Under the 'income from property' part of the Return there are also spaces for you to report your income under the Rent-a-room Scheme or from letting out property abroad.

The amount of interest earned during the year on your bank deposit account can be obtained from your bank statements. Most banks credit interest half-yearly at the end of each June and December. If you receive your interest at more frequent intervals or had a large sum on deposit for short fixed periods you must make sure that the interest from all your accounts is reported on the Tax Return. Where tax has been deducted from your bank interest you should enter the name of the bank, show the gross amount of interest before deduction of tax, the tax deducted and the net amount received.

Use the same section and procedure for reporting any building society interest received. You can normally obtain this information from your pass book. If you have an account which pays interest monthly you will need to enter the total of all your monthly receipts in the tax year.

Remember, when completing the sections on your Tax Return for National Savings, bank, building society and other interest income, to distinguish between interest where tax has been taken off at source from interest where no such deduction for tax has been made.

Dividends on your shareholdings come with counterfoils. These should always be kept. You can then list the dividends on the Tax Return. Alternatively you can just enter the total of all your dividends and tax credits during the year on the Tax Return and send in a separate listing with the Return.

The same procedure as that for dealing with your dividends should be followed where you are receiving fixed-interest payments and income from UK Unit Trusts from which tax is deducted at source. If you are fortunate enough to be receiving income from a Trust, the Trustees will send you a certificate showing your income each year. You

108 COMPLETING THE RETURN

Income from savings and investments - year to 5 April 1994

See note 26 for income you do not need to include. If you have joint savings and investments see note 27.

Complete this section if you received any interest, dividends from shares, income from unit trusts or other investment income. Even if the income was reinvested (ie not actually paid out to you) you must still give details. **If you received income from a jointly owned investment or a joint savings account, give only your share of the income.**

The first £70 of interest on National Savings Ordinary Accounts is exempt from tax, but must still be included here.

National Savings
Give the amounts you received, as shown on your statement. In the case of Capital Bonds, give the interest added to the Capital Bonds, as shown on your statement.

Ordinary Account	£
Investment Account	£ 250
Deposit Bonds	£ 190
Income Bonds	£
Capital Bonds	£

First Option Bonds
Give the amount you received as shown on your tax certificate

Net interest after tax	Tax deducted	Gross interest before tax
£ 225	£ 75	£ 300
£	£	£
£	£	£

Your bank or building society should be able to supply the details you need, but see note 28.

Do not forget to include interest from current accounts and accounts closed during the year.

Income from other UK banks, building societies and deposit takers
Name of the bank, building society, savings bank or deposit taker. Tick box if you have registered to have interest paid gross

Name	Interest after tax (leave blank if no tax was deducted)	Tax deducted (leave blank if no tax was deducted)	Gross interest
FIELDGATE BANK PLC	£120	£40	£160
FIELDGATE BUILDING SOCIETY	£375	£125	£500
	£	£	£
	£	£	£
	£	£	£
	£	£	£

Include interest on Government stocks (gilts), bonds, loans to individuals etc. See note 29.

Other interest you receive in the UK
Give the source of the interest

Source	Interest after tax (leave blank if no tax was deducted)	Tax deducted (leave blank if no tax was deducted)	Gross interest
3½% WAR LOAN	£	£	£60
	£	£	£
	£	£	£

Notes
Enter the figures shown on your dividend voucher.

If there is not enough space put the details on a separate sheet

Dividends from shares in UK companies
Do not include income from trusts, loan stock, dividends from overseas companies or stock dividends.

Name of the company	Tax credit	Dividend
JONES PLC	£ 20	£ 80
BROWN PLC	£ 16	£ 64
KEMP PLC	£ 32	£128
	£	£

Stock dividends
If you took up an offer of shares in place of a cash dividend (a 'stock dividend'), give the 'appropriate amount in cash' notified by the company in the dividend column.

Name of the company	Notional tax credit	Dividend
	£	£
	£	£
	£	£
	£	£

These figures should be on your unit trust voucher. If you have not received one, ask the unit trust manager. If there is not enough space put the details on a separate sheet

Income from UK unit trusts
Complete this if you received income from unit trusts, including income reinvested in units. If your voucher shows a tax credit, give the tax credit and the dividend. If your voucher shows tax deducted, give the tax deducted and the gross income.

Give the name of each unit trust	Tax credit or tax deducted	Dividend	Gross income
FIELDGATE EUROPEAN TRUST	£ 9	£36	£ 45
FIELDGATE U.K. GROWTH TRUST	£24	£96	£120
	£	£	£
	£	£	£

should enter the gross amount in the space provided in the Return. There is a box to tick if any trust income was only taxed at 20% (or carried a 20% tax credit).

The final section in your Tax Return dealing with your income requires you to report the maintenance or alimony payments you received in the year.

Outgoings

The next sections of the Return are to a large extent devoted to your borrowings, the interest paid on these loans, and your pension contributions. The purposes for which you can take out a loan and get tax relief on the interest are set out in Chapter 3. Make sure you attach to the Tax Return any certificate of interest paid, where this is relevant. Put a tick in the box on the Tax Return if you are married and want to vary the way that mortgage tax relief is split between you and your spouse.

Mortgage or loan for main home

See note 38. Do not include interest on overdrafts or credit cards, or home improvement loans taken out after 5 April 1988.

Complete this section if you paid interest in 1993-94 on a mortgage or other loan to buy your main home in the UK. Also complete this section if you paid interest on a loan which you took out before 6 April 1988 to:
- improve your main home or
- buy or improve the main home of your divorced or separated husband/wife or of certain relatives.

See note 39.

Joint mortgages with someone who is not your husband/wife
Tick here and give details below only for your share of the mortgage.

Husband and wife: change in interest relief split
If you are married and you and your husband/wife want to change the way mortgage interest relief is split between you, tick here and you will be sent a form on which you can do this.

If you had more than one loan during the year, for example if you moved and paid off a loan, give details of all loans. (On a separate sheet of paper if necessary)

Details of loan
Give details of each advance or loan separately. If the loan is not from a building society and you do not have mortgage interest relief at source enclose a form MIRAS 5, or other certificate of interest paid from your lender.

Name of lender
FIELDGATE BUILDING SOCIETY

Account number
F 23792

Tick here if not in MIRAS

Date loan started 08/10/1993
if after 6 April 1993

If you paid off the loan during the year
Address of the property

92 CHURCH STREET
FIELDGATE
TA6 3DF

Date loan paid off 08/10/1993

The following part of the Return asks you to provide information on interest payments on a loan taken out either to acquire property which you are letting out or for one of the other purposes mentioned in Chapter 3 where the interest is tax deductible.

Then comes the part of the Return for you to enter details of your retirement annuity payments and personal pension premiums. More information has to be given if you are an employee. Information about other deductions from your income come next. These include maintenance or alimony payments, private medical insurance premiums, Gift Aid donations, covenants to charity and payments for vocational-training. If you are over 60 and pay premiums for private medical insurance you need to give information about your insurer and your premiums paid during the tax year. If you are liable to tax at the higher rate of 40% you should obtain a certificate from your insurer certifying the premiums paid during the year to 5 April 1994. This certificate should be sent to yor Inspector of Taxes along with the Return.

Payments you make under either Deed of Covenant or the Gift Aid scheme should be entered on the Return after deduction of tax at the basic rate. For all your other covenanted payments you should enter the gross amounts paid in the year on the Return Form.

Private medical insurance for people aged 60 or over

If you would like more details ask your Tax Office for "Tax Relief for Private Medical Insurance" (leaflet IR103).

Complete this if you paid private medical insurance premiums for someone aged 60 or over (including you and/or your husband/wife) under a contract that was eligible for tax relief. If you wish to claim tax relief at the higher rate, please ask your insurer for a certificate of premiums paid in 1993-94 and then send it to your Tax Office.

Name of insurer

See note 46. Basic rate relief is given at source: give the amount you actually paid.

Name of insurer	FIELDGATE PROVIDENT ASSOCIATION	
Contract number	FPA 7297	Net amount paid in 1993-94 £450

If you made "Gift Aid" donations give the amounts you actually paid to each charity. Use a separate sheet of paper if necessary.

Gift aid donations		Net amount paid in 1993-94
Name of charity	FIELDGATE HOME FOR THE DEAF	£800

Give the amounts you actually paid to each charity. Use a separate sheet of paper if necessary. See note 47.

Covenants to charity		Net amount paid in 1993-94
Name of charity	FIELDGATE PARISH CHURCH	£25

Capital Gains

Every time you buy or sell shares or securities your broker sends you a contract note. Do not lose these as you will need them to complete this part of the Return. In order that any Capital Gains Tax due from you can be calculated, enter on the Return details of all the assets you sold during the tax year. Even if you think a profit on sale is exempt from tax, still report the sale in this section. Where your total chargeable gains, before losses, are less than £5,800 and the total proceeds of all your sales during the year are under £11,600 all you need to do is tick the box right at the start of the capital gains section on page 10 of the Return. You do not need to give any further details.

Allowances

As I mentioned earlier on in this chapter, the allowances

ALLOWANCES

section is for the current year to 5 April 1995 and should be completed with this in mind. All the various personal allowances which you can claim are set out in this section of the Return Form. In each case there is a space for you to enter the information the Inland Revenue need to tell you whether you are entitled to be given an allowance. You will be well advised to look through each section carefully.

Every individual, resident in the United Kingdom, is entitled to a personal allowance. A man can claim the married couple's allowance if he is married and lives with his wife for all or part of the tax year. Higher personal and married couple's allowances are given to a pensioner whose income is below a specified annual limit.

Allowances to be claimed by married men.
Married couple's allowance

You can only claim if you can tick one of these two boxes.

See note 56.

Tick the relevant box to claim

You are living with your wife. ✓

Give your wife's full name

SARAH LOUISE SMITH

You separated from your wife before 6 April 1990 but are still married to her and have wholly maintained her since the separation with voluntary payments for which you are not entitled to any tax relief.

If you married after 5 April 1993 give the date of your marriage

The next parts of this section deal with the allocation of the married couple's allowance, the transfer of surplus allowances to a wife, the circumstances when a wife can claim the additional personal allowance if she has a child living with her, and the widow's bereavement allowance. All of these were dealt with in Chapter 2.

The conditions which need to be satisfied before the additional personal allowance can be claimed are not identical for men and women. There are also special rules for unmarried couples living together. A widow with a child living with her at home will complete this part of the Tax Return as follows:

Notes

See notes 59 and 60.

If you have a child and are single, separated, divorced or widowed

You may be able to claim the additional personal allowance if you have a child living with you for at least part of the year and you are single, separated, divorced or widowed at some time during the year.

Give the child's date of birth 06/08/1977

Give the name of the youngest child for whom you can claim

BARBARA SMITH

Tick here if the child lives with you.

If the child was 16 or over on 6 April 1994 and in full-time education or training give the name of the university, college or school or the type of training.

FIELDGATE TECHNICAL COLLEGE

Use the following part of this section where you make a claim for the special blind person's allowance.

The final part of the Return asks for your personal details

such as your National Insurance Number, date of birth, marital status and your new address if you have recently moved.

Penalties

The Inland Revenue will impose interest and penalties if you omit to tell your tax office about some source of income or capital gain or fail to submit your Tax Returns promptly. The Inland Revenue are likely to levy an interest charge on Income Tax or Capital Gains Tax charged on an assessment, which has to be raised to collect the tax due on new sources of income, existing sources of income where no notice of appeal was made against an inadequate estimated assessment, or capital gains and you have not sent in your Tax Return by 31 October following the end of the tax year. If you are unable to submit your Return by this date, at least provide your Inspector of Taxes with sufficient information to enable him to raise a reasonable estimated assessment.

Making an incomplete or incorrect Tax Return or statement is also a serious offence which will lead to the levy of a penalty. The maximum penalties which are prescribed are:

Offence	*Penalty*
Failure to notify the Inspector of Taxes of each separate source of taxable income or liability to Capital Gains Tax within one year after the end of the tax year in which the income or gains arise	The tax payable on the relevant income or capital gains
Failure to complete a Tax Return	£300, plus a possible extra £60 a day. Where the failure continues beyond the end of the tax year after that in which the Return was issued the penalty is increased to 100% of the tax payable based on the Return
Making or submitting an incorrect Return, Account, Statement or Declaration	The amount of tax lost by the Inland Revenue
Assisting a taxpayer in making an incorrect Return or Account	Up to £3,000

PENALTIES 113

The Inland Revenue usually charge a penalty below the maximum limit. This depends on the seriousness of the offence and other circumstances. In addition, interest will also be charged from the date when the tax was normally due.

13

ASSESSMENTS AND REPAYMENT CLAIMS

If you ignore an assessment of demand sent to you by the Inland Revenue, the end result can come as an unpleasant surprise. Your responsibilities as a taxpayer are not just confined to completing your Tax Return each year. It is also important you understand what action you need to take whenever you receive an assessment and how to claim any repayment due to you.

Appeals
Each assessment sent to you will tell you how long you have in which to appeal against it. This time limit is usually 30 days. If you are late in dealing with the Return you run the risk of assessments being sent to you by the Inland Revenue which require some action within this appeal period. Providing you complete your Tax Return promptly it is less likely that any assessments you receive will be inaccurate.

The Inland Revenue have a special Form 64–7 for making an appeal against an assessment. One of these forms will usually be sent to you with each assessment. You are not bound to use it: if you prefer to make your objection in a letter this will do. What is important is that your appeal should clearly state the reasons why you disagree with the assessment. This will usually be because the Inland Revenue have estimated your income or business profits in the absence of your Tax Return or accounts. Where the assessment is excessive you should say so in your appeal. Alternatively, if it is not in accordance with information already sent, or to be provided, to the Inland Revenue then this will be the basis of your appeal. Wherever possible try and send the Inland Revenue the missing Return or outstanding information as soon as you can.

Inevitably the incorrect assessment shows you owe some tax. Where you think this is more than the amount which will ultimately be payable you should request that collection of the excess be postponed. Do this at the same time as your appeal. You must specify your reasons why you want all or part of the tax charged on the assessment postponed. Unless an application for postponement is made all the tax will be due and payable on the date shown on the assessment.

The majority of appeals are eventually settled by agreement between the taxpayer and the Inland Revenue. The assessment will then be adjusted to the agreed figures. There are occasions when agreement cannot be reached. The procedure for resolving your appeal starts with a hearing before the General Tax Commissioners. It can then move on to the Courts and ultimately to the House of Lords.

Should you ever reach the stage of receiving notification of a hearing of an appeal before the General Commissioners you ignore it at your peril. This is because the Commissioners have the power to determine your appeal. Unless you are represented at the hearing you can end up paying more than the true amount of tax due on the assessment.

Repayment claims

There are a number of situations which can lead to a tax refund. This can simply arise because you have paid more tax than you should have done. Alternatively, perhaps your business had a bad year and made a loss. A repayment would be due to you by setting the loss against other income on which tax had already been paid. In these situations the Inland Revenue will send your refund as soon as they receive a request for repayment from you.

There are also those taxpayers whose income mainly comes from investments. When they come to claim their personal allowances they will usually end up receiving an income tax repayment.

Illustration

A single woman had an income from dividends of £1,440 net during 1993/94. She also received building society interest of £1,725 and her earnings from a part-time employment were £1,300.

	Gross Income £	Tax Suffered £
Casual earnings	1,300	
Dividends		360.00
Building society interest	2,300	575.00
	5,400	935.00

Less: Personal allowance	3,445
Taxable income	£1,955

Tax thereon:

£1,955 at 20%	391.00
1993/94 Repayment	£544.00

Repayment supplement

Whenever the Inland Revenue make a refund to you they have to work out whether to supplement it by a payment of interest. The rate is identical to that used in working out interest on overdue tax, currently at 5.5%. The supplement is not taxable. It is calculated from one of two dates, whichever is the later. The first is the end of the tax year following the one for which the repayment is due. The second is the end of the year of assessment in which the tax was paid.

Remission of tax

There are occasions when the Inland Revenue does not act promptly after it receives your Tax Return or other information about a change in your circumstances. Where there is no response from the tax office it is not unreasonable for you to believe that your affairs are in order. If you were subsequently faced with a large demand which had built up through this sort of oversight it could cause you considerable hardship.

In recognition of this the Inland Revenue will not collect all the arrears of tax which have built up because of a failure to make proper and timely use of information supplied by the taxpayer. The amount you are let off depends on the size of your income when you are notified of the arrears. At present the following table applies:

Gross Income	Remit	Collect
up to £15,500	All	None
£15,501 to £18,000	75%	25%
£18,001 to £22,000	50%	50%
£22,001 to £26,000	25%	75%
£26,001 to £40,000	10%	90%
over £40,000	None	All

Normal dates for tax payments
For the tax year 1993/94 these are:

Type of Assessment	Date of Payment
Income Tax and Class 4 National Insurance contributions on business profits	Half on 1 January 1994 half on 1 July 1994
Income Tax on rents and untaxed interest	1 January 1994
Higher rate on taxed investment income	1 December 1994
Capital Gains Tax	1 December 1994

Interest on overdue tax

If you delay paying your tax after it is due you face the prospect of being charged interest. The rate is worked out on a set formula. It is Bank Base rate plus 2.5%, reduced by the basic rate of tax. At the time of going into print the rate is 5.5%. The interest is calculated from the due date up until payment. You cannot claim tax relief on the interest. Except where an appeal is given against an assessment the due date will either be one of those in the preceding section in this chapter or 30 days after the assessment is issued if that is later.

For assessments under appeal interest is charged from the earlier of the due date or the date in the following table depending on the type of assessment. For the 1993/94 tax year these are:

Type of Assessment	Applicable Date
Income Tax on business profits, Rents or untaxed interest	1 July 1994
Higher rate on taxed investment income	1 June 1995
Capital Gains Tax	1 June 1995

14

ELECTIONS AND CLAIMS – TIME LIMITS

You will already have gathered that certain options available to you as a taxpayer are dependent on you submitting an election or claim to the Inspector of Taxes. As these will usually involve a saving in tax it is important to appreciate that all elections or claims must be submitted within prescribed time limits. This chapter brings together those elections and claims which are most likely to concern you. It also sets out the time available during which they must be submitted to the Inspector of Taxes. It is by no means exhaustive.

Election/Claim	**Time Limit**
Chapter 2 – Personal Allowances and Reliefs	
By a wife to receive one half of the married couple's allowance	Before the start of the tax year for which it is to have effect
An election for the married couple's allowance to be deducted wholly from a wife's total income	As above
A subsequent election by a husband to take back one half of the married couple's allowance	As above
Withdrawal of any of the above elections	As above
Claim to the various personal allowances detailed in the chapter	Six years after the end of the year of assessment
Transfer of excess allowances between husband and wife	Six years after the end of the year of assessment
Chapter 3 – Interest Payments and Other Outgoings	
Election for mortgage interest payable by one spouse to be treated as if payable by the other spouse, or revocation of such an election	Within 12 months after the end of the year of assessment

Chapter 6 – The Self-Employed

Claim for the second and third years of assessment of a new business to be revised to the actual profits earned in those years	Seven years after the end of the second year of assessment
Creating a separate pool to work out the capital allowances on an asset with a short life expectancy	Within two years of the year of acquisition
Notification of a claim to capital allowances on expenditure on plant and machinery	Within two years after the end of the chargeable period in which the expenditure is incurred
Relief for losses sustained in the year of assessment	Two years after the end of the year of assessment in which the loss is made
Relief for the loss sustained in the preceding year of assessment	Three years after the end of the year of assessment in which the loss is made
Relief for the loss in the first four years of assessment of a new business to be given against the income of the three preceding years of assessment	Two years after the end of the year of assessment in which the loss occurred

Chapter 7 – Personal Pensions

Personal pension premiums to be treated as paid in the preceding year of assessment	5 July in the year of assessment after that in which payment was made
Retirement annuity premiums to be treated as paid in the preceding year of assessment	5 April in the year of assessment in which payment was made

Chapter 8 – Investment Income

An election to opt out of the Rent-a-room relief for a particular tax year, or withdrawal of an election	Within one year after the end of the year of assessment
An election for the alternative basis of Rent-a-room relief, or revocation of an election	Within one year after the end of the year of assessment
Claim for the third year of assessment on a source of untaxed interest to be adjusted to the actual interest earned in the year	Six years after the end of the year of assessment
Claim for relief under the Business Expansion Scheme	Two years after the end of the year of assessment in which the shares were issued or, if later, 28 months after the company begins to trade

Declaration by a married couple that their beneficial interest in joint property and the income arising from it are unequal	The date of the declaration

Chapter 9 – The Family Unit

An election for the income tax treatment of maintenance payments under obligations which existed on 15 March 1988 to change to the basis appropriate to arrangements made since then	By the payer within one year after the end of the first year of assessment for which it is to apply. The election cannot be revoked

Chapter 11 – Capital Gains Tax

Claim to the capital loss where the value of an asset becomes negligible	The loss arises on the date of claim although, in practice, a two-year period is allowed from the time the asset became of negligible value
Claim for the loss on shares that were originally subscribed for in an unquoted trading company to be set against income in the year of loss, or the following year	Two years after the end of the year of assessment in which the relief is taken
An election for the capital gains on disposals of assets you owned on 31 March 1982 to be worked out by reference to their values on that date, ignoring original costs	Within two years after the end of the tax year in which the first disposal of an asset you owned on 31 March 1982 takes place
Claim for the 6 April 1965 value to be substituted in a calculation of the capital gain arising on the sale of an asset held at that date	Two years from the end of the year of assessment in which the disposal is made
An election to determine which of your homes is to be regarded as your principal residence for Capital Gains Tax purposes	Two years from the date when two or more properties are eligible
Claim to exemption from Capital Gains Tax on the disposal of a residence occupied by a dependent relative	Six years from the end of the year in which the gain arose
Claim to roll-over relief on the disposal of business assets	Six years after the end of the year of assessment
Claim to a reduction in the deferred gain on assets acquired in the period 31 March 1982 to 5 April 1988	Two years from the end of the year of assessment in which the disposal takes place

15

INHERITANCE TAX

Inheritance Tax was introduced in 1986 as the successor to Capital Transfer Tax. Not only might Inheritance Tax be payable on transfers of gifts you make during your lifetime, but it is also due on the value of your estate on death. Husband and wife are treated as separate individuals, and both are entitled to the various exemptions. Inheritance Tax is far from straightforward. What follows is a brief outline. The Tax is administered by the Capital Taxes Office, to whom any Returns should be submitted.

Potentially exempt transfers

The most significant feature of Inheritance Tax is the concept of a potentially exempt transfer (PET). This is:

(1) An outright gift to an individual.
(2) A gift into an accumulation-and-maintenance settlement.
(3) A gift into a settlement for the benefit of a disabled person.
(4) A gift into an interest in possession trust.
(5) The termination of an interest in possession settlement where the settled property passes to an individual, an accumulation-and-maintenance settlement, or a trust for the benefit of a disabled person.

No tax is payable providing the donor lives for at least seven years after making the gift. A form of tapering relief applies where death occurs within seven years. The amount of Inheritance Tax is then calculated at the rates which apply at the date of death as shown in the following table:

Number of Years between Gift and Death	% of Tax Payable
Not more than 3	100
Between 3 and 4	80
Between 4 and 5	60
Between 5 and 6	40
Between 6 and 7	20

Gifts with reservation

If you make a gift but continue to enjoy some benefit from it, the property or asset you have given away is likely to be treated as yours until either the date when you cease to enjoy any benefit from the gift or your death. This is a 'gift with reservation'. For example, you give your house to your children but continue to live there, rent free. Your house would then be counted as part of your estate and the seven year period would not start until you either moved home or began to pay a commercial rent.

Lifetime gifts

If you make a gift during your lifetime which is not a potentially exempt transfer it will attract liability to Inheritance Tax at one half of the rates which apply on death. An example of such a lifetime gift is a transfer into a discretionary trust.

Exemptions

The main exemptions applicable to individuals are:

(1) Transfers between husband and wife.
(2) Gifts up to £3,000 in any one tax year. Any part of the exemption which is left over can be carried forward to the following year only. For example, if your total transfers came to £1,500 during 1992/93 you could have given away as much as £4,500 during 1993/94 all within your annual exemption limit. However, if your gifts totalled £3,000 in 1992/93, you would be limited to £3,000 in 1993/94 as well.
(3) Gifts to any one person up to £250 per person in each tax year. Where the total amount given to any one individual exceeds this limit no part comes within this exemption.
(4) Marriage gifts. The amount you can give away depends on your relationship to the bride or groom, as follows:

	£
By either parent	5,000
By a grandparent or great grandparent	2,500
By any other person	1,000

(5) Regular gifts out of income which form part of your normal expenditure.
(6) Gifts and bequests to charities without limit.
(7) Gifts to 'qualifying' political parties without limit.

Miscellaneous aspects

Business assets, including shares you own in a family company, qualify for special relief for Inheritance Tax purposes. Put simply, this relief involves reducing the taxable values of the transfers of specific types of property, as follows:

By 100%

> An interest in the whole or part of a business.
>
> Holdings over 25% in Unquoted and Unlisted Securities Market companies.

By 50%

> Controlling holdings in Fully Quoted companies.
>
> Holdings of 25% or less, without control, in Unquoted and Unlisted Securities Market companies.
>
> Certain assets owned by partners, or controlling shareholders, and used in their businesses.

Agricultural property and woodlands also qualify for similar forms of relief. Inheritance Tax can also apply in varying ways to different types of trusts.

Rates of tax

Each taxable gift or transfer is not considered in isolation in calculating how much tax is payable on it. In working out how much is payable, previous taxable transfers are taken into account. This is because the tax due on each chargeable gift or the value of your estate on death is dependent upon the cumulative value of all other chargeable transfers in the seven years leading up to the date of the next chargeable transfer. The rates payable on death from 10 March 1992 are:

Band	Rate
£	%
0–150,000	0
Over 150,000	40

These rates also apply to all lifetime gifts or transfers within three years of death. Inheritance Tax payable on PETS more than three years before but within seven years of death is determined by the first table in this chapter.

The limit of £150,000 on chargeable transfers taxable at a nil rate is increased each year in the same way as the main personal Income Tax allowances.

Illustration

Mrs Brown, a widow, died on 30 September 1993 leaving her entire estate to her daughter. She did not make any gifts in the seven years leading up to her death. Her assets and unpaid bills on her death were:

Assets	Value	
	£	£
Flat	120,000	
Household effects	2,000	
Car	4,000	
Building society account	20,000	
Shares	27,500	
Current account	500	
		174,000
Less: Allowable Deductions		
Funeral expenses	920	
Income Tax	500	
Telephone bill	50	
Electricity bill	60	
		1,530
Net Value of Estate		**£172,470**

Inheritance Tax Payable	
On first £150,000	Nil
On next £22,470 at 40%	£8,988
	£8,988

The tax is payable out of Mrs Brown's estate by the executors of her will.

Intestacy

If you die without having made a will your estate will be divided up under the statutory intestacy rules. If you are married and survived by both your spouse and children, your spouse is entitled to a statutory legacy of £125,000. This increases to £200,000 if there are no children but you are survived by specific relatives.

The present intestacy rules can best be summarized as follows:

Unmarried Individual

Survived by	Division of Estate
(1) Children	Divided equally between them
(2) No children but parents	Shared equally between them
(3) Neither children nor parents, but brothers and sisters	Divided equally between them
(4) No children, parents, brothers, sisters but grandparents	Shared equally between them
(5) Only aunts and uncles	Divided equally between them
(6) No relatives as listed above	Estate passes to Crown

Married Individual

Particular Circumstances	Division
(1) Estate amounts to less than £125,000	All to spouse
(2) Estate exceeds £125,000 and there are children	Spouse is entitled to first £125,000 and a life interest in half the remainder. The balance is divided between the children
(3) Estate is worth less than £200,000 and there are no children	All to spouse
(4) Estate comes to more than £200,000, the couple have no children but parents are still alive	Spouse receives first £200,000 and half the remainder absolutely. The parents share the rest
(5) As in (4) above, parents are dead, but there are brothers and sisters	As in (4) above but the balance is shared between the brothers and sisters instead of the parents
(6) The only survivor is the spouse	All to spouse

16

TAX-SAVING HINTS

There are many factors you should bear in mind before you take any decisions about reorganizing your finances. I am sure we all regard a saving in tax as a bit like the icing on the cake. Nevertheless, opportunities to save tax should never be considered in isolation.

First and foremost comes your own personal circumstances. Perhaps your wife has a low taxable income and you are wondering whether to transfer some investments into her own name so she can benefit from her full personal allowance. These investments will then belong to her. Most couples will continue to enjoy the benefits from their saving in tax for many years to come. Regrettably, some couples will split up. While no couple ever wants to contemplate that their marriage will break down, the prospect of this happening should, at the very least, be borne in mind in any tax planning exercise. The same applies where you are thinking about gifts to your children. They have been known to subsequently fall out with their parents.

When it comes to investments remember that you will sometimes need to be locked into an investment for a number of years before you can receive the full tax benefits. A typical example of this sort of investment is one under the new Enterprise Investment Scheme. You should judge the merits of any investment from all angles. Sometimes it will be best to steer clear of investments which are inflexible. You could end up endangering your family's financial security. The same applies to those investments which carry a high degree of risk.

In the fast moving world in which we live you must keep your finances under constant review. Although tax rates have been substantially unchanged for a number of years you must be ready to adjust your finances to take account of reductions or increases in the various taxes. When it comes to Inheritance Tax remember it will be the law at some time in the future on your death which will determine the tax payable by your Executors.

Personal allowances and reliefs

Under Independent Taxation every man and woman, single or married, is entitled to the personal allowance. For a variety of reasons there will be many wives who are unable to take full advantage of their personal allowance. This is where the husband should consider transferring capital to his wife in order to generate taxable income for her.

With differing rates of personal and married couple's age allowances for pensioners in the 65–74 and over 74 age brackets, elderly couples need to pay even more care and attention to their respective incomes. Of particular help to the elderly couple is that the annual income limit of £14,200 above which the personal age allowance is restricted no longer depends on their joint income. Whether an elderly spouse can claim the personal age allowance depends solely on his or her income. They must also remember that the amount of the married couple's age allowance due to the husband is governed by the age of the elder spouse.

Do not forget to consider whether the new rules governing the transfer of the married couple's allowance between husband and wife can save you tax. The allowance can now be deducted wholly from the wife's total income, instead of the husband's income.

Interest payments and other outgoings

As a first time buyer, or whenever you move home, try and take full advantage of the rules for mortgage interest tax relief. The maximum loan limit is £30,000 and applies to any one home rather than to each borrower. As a further attraction the profit on sale of your home is exempt from Capital Gains Tax.

For those of you who are in the habit of making donations to charity there are advantages of making these under either Deed of Covenant or the Gift Aid Scheme. Charities are able to claim repayment of the tax you must deduct at the basic rate. If you are liable to tax at the top rate of 40% you will also gain as you are allowed to deduct payments under the Gift Aid Scheme and Charitable Covenants in calculating your higher rate liabilities.

Earnings from employment

If you are fortunate enough to have the use of a company car, keep an eye on your annual business mileage. During recent years there have been substantial increases in the scale of taxable benefits. As a result the number of miles you travel each year on business can sometimes have a significant impact on the Income Tax payable on this benefit. From 6 April 1994 a new system applies in working out the taxable value of this benefit. It is based on the list price of your company car. Further information can be found in the *Budget Measures* supplement at the end of the book.

You face a further taxable benefit if it is your employer's policy to meet the cost of petrol for private motoring. Where your private mileage is low it is likely you will be better off to pay for your own petrol for non-business travel.

To attract and retain staff, employers will usually incorporate at least some of the benefits with a favourable tax treatment in their remuneration packages. Top of the list comes a company pension plan, closely followed by a company car, private medical insurance, and Luncheon Vouchers or a staff canteen. An interest free or subsidized loan, child care facilities, share options, and Profit Related Pay are among the perks generally offered by larger companies.

The self-employed

Make sure you claim all the expenses of running your business in your annual accounts. Where appropriate pay your wife a salary for the secretarial or other assistance she gives you. You should consider taking your wife into partnership where she helps you in your business and your annual profits are such that the top slice is liable to tax at the higher 40% rate. This is definitely an area where you should seek professional advice. If you are thinking about buying plant and machinery or, for example, a new car then it is better to do so towards the end of your accounting year rather than early on in the following year. You benefit from the capital allowances due on the expenditure at an earlier date.

If you have incurred a loss in your business look at all the options available for claiming the tax relief due on the loss. You may well find that one or other of the different alternatives available produces a bigger Income Tax repayment particularly when the tax-free repayment supplement paid by the Inland Revenue is taken into account. Remember to make sure that the formal loss relief claim is submitted to your Inspector of Taxes within the permitted time limit.

Personal pensions and other investments

A review of your pension arrangements should be at the top of your list in any financial planning exercise. Pension Schemes offer, perhaps, the greatest scope for tax saving and tax planning, including:

Replacement of your income when you retire.
Tax relief on premiums at your top rate of tax.
No UK tax payable by Pension Funds.
Tax-free lump sum on retirement.
Tax-deductible death benefits for your family.
Death benefits free of Inheritance Tax.

For these reasons you should certainly consider whether your existing pension arrangements are sufficient for your own and your family's needs, both now and in the future.

If for some reason you have been unable to make your maximum pension contributions in previous years, you are allowed to carry forward the unused relief for up to six years. Where you are still paying premiums into a retirement annuity taken out before the beginning of July 1988 it may be better for you to continue with this policy rather than start a personal pension plan. However, do not overlook the higher annual contribution limits into a personal pension compared with a retirement annuity. When you come to consider whether to make an election for the premiums paid in a tax year to be treated as if paid in the preceding tax year, remember the time limit for making the election for a personal pension premium is more generous than that where the premium is paid into a retirement annuity.

Alternatively, if you are a member of your employer's pension scheme, consider whether there is scope for enhancing your benefits by the payment of Additional Voluntary Contributions.

Whenever you can, make the most of the various investment opportunities where the return is tax free, such as National Savings Certificates, TESSAs, PEPs and Friendly Societies. If you are a non-taxpayer, get a special form from a Bank, Building Society, Post Office or Tax Office so that you can receive your Bank or Building Society interest with no deduction for tax. This option will be of considerable benefit to those pensioners, children and dependent married women who are not liable to Income Tax on their savings.

If you are letting furnished accommodation in your home you should consider whether you can benefit from the new Rent-a-room relief. Gross annual rents below £3,250 are exempt from tax. When your rents exceed £3,250 per annum you have a choice of two ways to work out your annual tax liability.

Capital Gains Tax

Even if some part of your annual Capital Gains Tax exemption – £5,800 for 1993/94 – is not utilized it cannot be carried forward to future years. The well-known practice of 'bed-and-breakfasting' shares under the simple procedure of sale and repurchase on consecutive days in the same Stock Exchange account is one way of realizing gains to use up your annual exemption limit. The same method can also be used to establish losses and reduce your net taxable gains in a tax year below the annual exemption limit. Do not forget that the excess of your chargeable gains over and above the exemption limit is charged at the tax rates which are appropriate when it is added to your taxable income. By realizing losses you may be able to substantially reduce your Capital Gains Tax liability particularly if you are a 40% tax payer.

Where it is to your advantage do not overlook making an election for the gains and losses on disposals of assets which you owned on 31 March 1982 to be calculated solely by reference to their market value at that date. The time limit for making the election is two years after the end of the tax year in which the first disposal of an asset you owned on 31 March 1982 takes place. If you have two homes you are allowed to make an election stipulating which of your homes you want to be regarded as your principal private residence for Capital Gains Tax purposes. The profit on a sale of this home will be exempt from tax. This election must be made within two years from the date when two or more properties are eligible.

Inheritance Tax

Where you can afford to do so make use of the annual exemption of £3,000. It follows that a married couple can give away as much as £60,000 tax free over a 10 year period under this exemption alone. Alternatively, you could consider using the exemption to pay premiums on a life policy written in Trust for the next generations. In this way the lump sum payable on your death under the policy will pass free of tax to your nominated beneficiaries.

Gifts of a more substantial amount should be made as early as possible to give you the best chance of surviving the seven year period. When making gifts make sure you retain no benefit from the gifted property.

If your spouse is adequately provided for, leave assets in your will equivalent in value to the amount of the nil rate band (currently £150,000) to other beneficiaries.

Illustration

A married couple have the following assets:

Husband	–	£300,000
Wife	–	£200,000

On the husband's death he leaves all his assets to his wife. No Inheritance Tax is payable. When the wife dies her executors will face an Inheritance Tax liability of £140,000 on her estate of £500,000 as follows:

On first	£150,000	Nil
On next	£350,000 @ 40%	£140,000
		£140,000

The beneficiaries of the wife's will receive £360,000.

Supposing, however, that the husband leaves £150,000 to beneficiaries other than his wife, and the balance of £150,000 to her. There would still be no Inheritance Tax payable on his death. The wife's estate of £350,000 would bear Inheritance Tax of £80,000 (£350,000 – £150,000 at 40%).

The beneficiaries receive a total amount from the two estates of £420,000 (£150,000 from the husband and £270,000 from the wife). This is some £60,000 more than under the couple's original wills.

Even if a will does not make use of all available reliefs, it may nevertheless be possible to do so by means of a Deed of Variation completed within two years of a death. In the above illustration, where the husband left all his assets to his wife, she could execute a Deed of Variation and pass assets worth £150,000 to the succeeding beneficiaries. These assets would be treated as passing under the husband's will thus taking advantage of his nil rate band. This is one of the more complicated areas of tax planning where you should always seek professional advice.

17

LOOKING AHEAD: SELF-ASSESSMENT AND SIMPLIFICATION OF PERSONAL TAX

The 1994 Finance Bill includes the legislation to implement the major reforms to the system for assessing personal tax announced by the then Chancellor, Mr. Lamont, in his March 1993 Budget. The main proposals will

- Give all taxpayers who complete Tax Returns for 1996/97 the option to work out their own liabilities to both Income Tax and Capital Gains Tax.

- Introduce a uniform set of dates for the payment of Income Tax and Capital Gains Tax with effect from 31 January 1998.

- Replace the existing 'preceding year' basis of assessment for the self-employed with the simpler 'current year' basis of assessment. This change will affect all businesses starting up after 5 April 1994. Existing businesses will move over to the new system from the 1997/98 tax year.

What follows in this chapter is an outline of the reforms so far announced.

SELF-ASSESSMENT

Tax Returns

Individuals will be required to send back their Tax Returns to their tax offices by the filing date. This will be 31 January following the end of the tax year or, if later, three months after the issue of the Return. The Return should include a self-assessment of the taxpayer's liability to Income Tax and Capital Gains Tax. Taxpayers who do not want to work out their own tax bill will not have to do so. They must then send back the completed Tax Return by 30 September following the end of the tax year or, if later, two months after the issue of the Return.

An automatic penalty of £100 will be imposed if a complete Return is not sent to the Inland Revenue on time. A further £100 penalty will be incurred if the failure continues for a further six months. If, for some reason, the failure goes beyond the first anniversary of the filing date, a penalty equivalent to the amount of the tax assessable for the year may be charged.

The Inland Revenue will be able to correct obvious errors or mistakes within nine months of the date after the Return is delivered. Taxpayers will have one year from the filing date of the Return in which to make any amendments to their Return. A broadly similar period will be given to the Inland Revenue in which they can give notice of their intention to enquire into a Return. If they do not do so, the Return will be final and conclusive unless the taxpayer makes an error or mistaken claim or, alternatively, the Inland Revenue makes a discovery that there has been an under-declaration of income or gains.

Procedures to protect revenue

Where a taxpayer has failed to deliver his Return by the due date, an officer of the Board will be able to make a determination to the best of his information and belief of the Income Tax and Capital Gains Tax due for the year of assessment. In such circumstances, the tax will be payable without appeal. However, the amount of tax so determined will automatically be superseded when the Return and self-assessment calculation are sent in.

As at present, the Inland Revenue will only be able to increase the liability for a previous year where an under-assessment is discovered and an officer of the Board has the power to correct it. Generally, the Inland Revenue will only be able to sustain a discovery assessment where there has been fraudulent or negligent conduct, or inadequate disclosure of the point at issue, by the taxpayer.

Payment of tax

Income Tax and Capital Gains Tax will normally be due on 31 January following the year of assessment. In addition, payments on account of Income Tax will be due on 31 January in the tax year and 31 July immediately following the year of assessment. These so-called 'interim payments' will normally be based on half each of the total Income Tax liability (less any tax deducted at source) for the preceding tax year. The taxpayer will be able to reduce payments where he believes that the tax due for the current year will be less than in the previous year. No payments on account will need to be made where the amount is below a threshold to be determined by the Treasury from time to time. The same applies where substantially all of the taxpayer's income is subject to deduction of tax at source, for example, under the PAYE system.

As at present, interest will be charged on tax which is paid late. Interest will be paid by the Inland Revenue on tax overpaid. If the tax liability for a year of assessment is outstanding by the following 28 February then a surcharge of 5% of the outstanding tax will be levied. A further 5% of any amount still outstanding at the following 31 July will also be charged.

Records
There will be a new requirement for taxpayers to keep records in support of their Returns. Trading records should be kept until the fifth anniversary of the filing date of the Return. Other records should be kept until the first anniversary of the filing date. If the Return is submitted late the records will need to be retained for a little while longer.

CURRENT YEAR BASIS OF ASSESSMENT

Introduction
In Chapter 6 I set out the way in which the profits of self-employed businesses are taxed. This is generally referred to as the 'previous year' basis of assessment. This is all set to change. Under the new 'current year' basis of assessment self-employed individuals will be charged on the profits made in the tax year. The profits shown by annual accounts drawn up to a date other than the end of the tax year – 'the basis period' – will continue to be regarded as those of the year to 5 April.

Illustration
An individual draws up his business accounts to 30 November each year. Under the new rules the profits disclosed by the accounts for the year to 30 November 1998 will be taxed in 1998/99.

For the first year of business the taxable profits will be limited to those arising in the period from commencement to 5 April. On cessation the profits for the final tax year will be those arising in the period from the end of the basis period assessed in the previous tax year.

Under these rules it is possible that some periods of account will feature for more than one tax year. However, over the lifetime of a business it is intended that the profits should be taxed in full, once and once only. Accordingly, any profits which are taxed more than once will be eligible for a special relief. Known as overlap relief, it will be given either when a business ceases or for any earlier tax year for which the basis period is longer than 12 months.

Illustration

A trader starts his business on 1 August 1997. His annual accounting date is 31 July. He makes the following profits:

Year to 31.07.1998	£15,000
Year to 31.07.1999	£18,000

The taxable profits for the first three tax years are:

Tax Year	Basis Period	Taxable Profit £
1997/98	01.08.1997 to 05.04.1998	10,000
1998/99	Year to 31.07.1998	15,000
1999/2000	Year to 31.07.1999	18,000

The business closes down on 30 April 2005. The taxable profit in the final period from 1 August 2004 to 30 April 2005 amounts to £12,000. The final tax year is 2005/06. The assessment will be on:

	£
Taxable profit in final period	12,000
Less: Overlap 01.08.1997 to 05.04.1998	10,000
Net assessment	£2,000

Special rules will apply when a business changes its accounting date. Apart from the first and last years of business the new system will aim to tax the profits of a 12 month period in each tax year.

Illustration

A trader commences business on 1 November 1997. He draws up his first accounts to 31 October 1998 which disclose a profit of £15,000. He then changes his accounting date to 31 December 1999. The accounts for the 14 month period show a taxable profit of £14,000. His basis periods and taxable profits for the opening years of assessment are:

Tax Year	Basis Period	Taxable Profit £
1997/98	01.11.1997 to 05.04.1998	6,250
1998/99	Year to 31.10.1998	15,000

The overlap period is from 01.11.1997 to 05.04.1998:

1999/2000	01.11.1998 to 31.12.1999 (14 months)	14,000
Less:	Overlap 01.11.1997 to 31.12.1997	2,500
Net assessment		£11,500

The overlap period was one of five months. As the accounting period from 1 November 1998 to 31 December 1999 is 14 months, the overlap relief is two months. The amount deducted from the assessment for 1999/2000 is ⅖ of the original overlap profit. Three months of overlap relief is then available either when the business ceases or for any subsequent tax year when the basis period is longer than 12 months.

Transitional arrangements

As part of the move over from the 'previous year' to 'current year' basis of assessment, special rules have been devised for those businesses in existence on 5 April 1994. These will determine the period for which profits are taxable for 1996/97. When a business continues to draw up its accounts to the same date each year the position is straightforward. The taxable profits will be half of those for the two year period ending in the 1996/97 tax year. Otherwise a 12 month average of the period starting after the basis period for 1995/96, and ending in 1996/97, will be used.

Illustration

A trader has been in business for many years. His annual accounting date is 5 April. In the years to 5 April 1996 and 1997 he makes taxable profits of £10,000 and £16,000 respectively. His assessment for 1996/97 will be on profits of £13,000 (one-half of the total profits for the two year period).

Illustration
Another trader has been in business since 1986. He has always prepared accounts to each 30 June. His profits for the year to 30 June 1995 amount to £10,000. However, he decides to change his accounting date to 31 March and draws up accounts for a 21 month period from 1 July 1995 to 31 March 1997. These disclose taxable profits of £23,000. In 1996/97 he will be taxed on profits of £12,000 as follows:

	£
12 months to 30.06.1995	10,000
21 months to 31.03.1997	23,000
33 months	£33,000
Taxable profits: £33,000 x $^{12}/_{33}$ =	£12,000

Many businesses will inevitably make up accounts for a period which straddles 5 April 1997. That part of the period which comes within the 1996/97 tax year will form part of the assessment for 1997/98. The profits of the part period of 1996/97 will rank for overlap relief.

Illustration
A trader prepares his accounts to 31 December each year. The basis period and taxable profits for 1997/98 are:

1997/98   01.01.1997 to 31.12.1997   £16,000

The period from 1 January 1997 to 5 April 1997 is an overlap period. Overlap relief of £4,000 will be due to the trader either when his business ceases or in a year for which the basis period is more than 12 months long.

The existing 'previous year' basis of assessment rules will continue to apply to any business which ceases before the new system comes in on 6 April 1997. The position is more complicated for businesses affected by the transitional arrangements and which cease during the two years to 5 April 1999.

The 1995 Finance Bill will contain legislation to protect the Exchequer against the loss of tax which may otherwise arise from attempts to take advantage of the transitional rules.

Losses

At present a business loss is set against your other taxable income for the same year. Any unused part of the loss can then be set against your taxable income in the subsequent year. The balance of the loss which is left over must be carried forward to be set against the profits from the same business in later years. Under the new rules loss relief that can be set against your other income will be allowed firstly against income of the same year and secondly against your taxable income of the preceding year.

Under the transitional arrangements losses arising in the basis period for 1996/97 will be relieved once in full.

Capital allowances

The chargeable period for capital allowances purposes will be the same as the period for which accounts are drawn up, instead of, as now, the year of assessment. This change takes place from the 1997/98 tax year. At the same time capital allowances will be treated as trading expenses and balancing charges as trading receipts.

Partnerships

From 1997/98 there is a major change to the taxation treatment of partnerships. At present an assessment is raised on the partnership in respect of the total taxable profits of the partnership for that tax year. From 1997/98 each individual partner's share of the profits will be assessed on him or her individually. Each partner's share will be allocated by reference to the period of account. All of the tax-deductible business expenses and capital allowances will still be allowed in arriving at the annual profits of a partnership.

Non-business income

Back in Chapter 8 I mentioned that interest not taxed at source is presently taxed in the special way similar to the income or profits from self-employment. The new 'current year' basis of assessment will also apply to other types of income, such as untaxed interest, presently dealt with under the 'previous year' basis of assessment. Beginning with the 1997/98 tax year the taxable income will be the income arising in the year. The transitional arrangements will also apply as part of the change to the new system.

TABLE 1

INLAND REVENUE EXPLANATORY BOOKLETS

No.	Title
IR 1	Extra Statutory Concessions
IR 14/15	Construction Industry Tax Deduction Scheme
IR 16	Income Tax: Share Acquisitions by Directors and Employees
IR 20	Residents and Non-Residents – Liability to Tax in the United Kingdom
IR 24	Class 4 National Insurance Contributions
IR 26	Income Tax Assessments on Business Profits – Changes of Accounting Date
IR 28	Tax and Your Business – Starting in Business
IR 33	Income Tax and School Leavers
IR 34	Income Tax: Pay As You Earn (PAYE)
IR 37	Income Tax and Capital Gains Tax: Appeals
IR 40	Income Tax: Conditions for getting a Sub-contractor's Tax Certificate
IR 41	Income Tax and the Unemployed
IR 42	Income Tax: Lay-Offs and Short-Time Work
IR 43	Income Tax and Strikes
IR 45	Income Tax, Capital Gains Tax and Inheritance Tax: What Happens When Someone Dies
IR 53	Thinking of Taking Someone On?
IR 56	Employed or Self-Employed? A Guide for Tax and National Insurance
IR 57	Thinking of Working for Yourself?
IR 58	Going to Work Abroad
IR 60	Income Tax and Students
IR 64	Giving to Charity: How Businesses can get Tax Relief
IR 65	Giving to Charity: How Individuals can get Tax Relief
IR 68	Income Tax – Accrued Income Scheme
IR 69	Expenses – Form P11D — How to Save Yourself Work
IR 71	PAYE: Inspection of Employers' and Contractors' Records
IR 72	Inland Revenue Investigations: The Examination of Business Accounts

IR 73	Inland Revenue Investigations: How Settlements are Negotiated
IR 75	Tax Reliefs for Charities
IR 78	Personal Pensions. A Guide for Tax
IR 80	Income Tax and Married Couples
IR 87	Rooms to Let – Income from letting Property
IR 89	Personal Equity Plans
IR 90	Independent Taxation – A Guide to Tax Allowances and Reliefs
IR 91	Independent Taxation: A Guide for Widows and Widowers
IR 92	Income Tax – A Guide for One-Parent Families
IR 93	Income Tax – A Guide to Separation, Divorce and Maintenance Payments
IR 95	Shares for Employees – Profit-Sharing Schemes
IR 97	Shares for Employees – SAYE Share Options
IR 99	Shares for Employees – Executive Share Options
IR 103	Tax Relief on Private Medical Insurance
IR 104	Tax and your Business – Simple Tax Accounts
IR 105	Tax and your Business – How your profits are taxed
IR 106	Tax and your Business – Capital Allowances for Vehicles and Machinery
IR 109	PAYE: Inspection of Employers' or Contractors' Records – How Settlements are Negotiated
IR 110	A Guide for People with Savings
IR 113	Gift Aid – A Guide for Donors and Charities
IR 114	TESSA – Tax-free interest for Taxpayers
IR 115	Tax and Childcare
IR 116	Guide for Sub-Contractor's with Tax Certificates
IR 117	Sub-Contractor's Guide to the Deduction Scheme
IR 119	Tax Relief for Vocational Training
IR 120	You and the Inland Revenue
IR 121	Income Tax and Pensioners
IR 123	Mortgage Interest Relief – Buying Your Home
IR 127	Are You Paying Too Much Tax on Your Savings?
IR 133	Income Tax and Company Cars from from 6 April 1994: a Guide for Employees
480	Income Tax – Notes on Expenses/Payments and Benefits for Directors and Certain Employees

P7/P8	Employers' Guides to PAYE
CGT 4	Capital Gains Tax – Owner-Occupied Houses
CGT 6	Capital Gains Tax – Retirement Relief on Disposal of a Business
CGT 11	Capital Gains Tax and Small Businesses
CGT 13	Capital Gains Tax – The Indexation Allowance for Quoted Shares
CGT 14	Capital Gains Tax: An Introduction
CGT 15	Capital Gains Tax: A Guide for Married Couples
CGT 16	Capital Gains Tax: Indexation Allowance – Disposals after 5 April 1988
IHT 3	An Introduction to Inheritance Tax

TABLE 2

FLAT RATE ALLOWANCES FOR SPECIAL CLOTHING AND THE UPKEEP OF TOOLS – 1993/94

(1) Fixed rate for all occupations

	£
Agricultural	60
Forestry	60
Quarrying	60
Brass and copper	85
Precious metals	60
Textile prints	50
Food	30
Glass	50
Railways	60
Uniformed prison officers	45
Uniformed bank employees	30
Uniformed police officers up to and including chief inspector	45

(2) Variable rate depending on category of occupation

Seamen	110/140
Iron mining	65/85
Iron and steel	40/50/105
Aluminium	40/50/85/110
Engineering	40/50/85/105
Shipyards	40/50/65/95
Vehicles	30/50/90
Particular engineering	40/50/85/105
Constructional engineering	40/50/65/95
Electrical and electricity supply	20/75
Textiles	50/70
Clothing	25/40
Leather	30/45
Printing	25/60/90
Building materials	30/45/70
Wood and furniture	40/65/75/95
Building	30/45/70/90
Heating	60/75/90
Public service	30/45

Notes

(a) The allowances are only available to manual workers who have to bear the cost of upkeep of tools and special clothing. Other employees, such as office staff, cannot claim them.

(b) Nurses may claim a fixed annual allowance of £18 to cover the cost of shoes and tights.

TABLE 3

RATES OF NATIONAL INSURANCE CONTRIBUTIONS FOR 1993/94

CLASS 1 Contributions for Employees

	Standard Rate On First £56.00	Standard Rate On Remainder	Contracted Out On First £56.00	Contracted Out On Remainder
Contributions levied on all weekly earnings if they reach £56.00 but do not exceed £420.00	2%	9%	2%	7%
If weekly earnings exceed £420.00	No Additional Contributions		No Additional Contributions	

Reduced Rate for Married Women and Widows with a Valid Election Certificate	3.85%

	£
Men over 65 and Women over 60	Nil
Lower Earnings Limit – Weekly	56
– Monthly	243
– Annually	2,912
Upper Earnings Limit – Weekly	420
– Monthly	1,820
– Annually	21,840

CLASS 2 Contributions for the Self-Employed

Weekly flat rate	5.55
Small earnings exception	3,140

CLASS 3 Voluntary Contributions

Weekly rate	5.45

CLASS 4 Contributions for the Self-Employed

6.3% of profits between £6,340 and £21,840

TABLE 4

VAT NOTICES AND LEAFLETS

No.	Title
700	The VAT Guide
700/ 1/92	Should I be Registered for VAT?
700/11/93	Cancelling Your Registration
700/12/93	Filling in your VAT Return
700/13A/93	VAT Publications
700/15/91	The Ins and Outs of VAT
700/21/91	Keeping Records and Accounts
700/26/92	Visits by VAT Officers
700/30/89	Default Surcharge Appeals
700/41/88	Late Registration: Penalties and Reasonable Excuse
700/42/93	Serious Mis-Declaration Penalty
700/43/93	Default Interest
700/45/93	How to Correct Errors you find on your VAT Returns
725	The Single Market
727	Choosing your Retail Scheme
727/7–15	How to Work Retail Schemes A–J
731	VAT: Cash Accounting
732	VAT: Annual Accounting
748	Extra Statutory Concessions

TABLE 5

CAPITAL GAINS TAX – THE INDEXATION ALLOWANCE

Starting month for Indexation

Month of disposal 1993

	Apr	May	Jun	Jul	Aug	Sept	Oct	Nov	Dec
1982									
Mar	.770	.776	.775	.771	.779	.786	.785	.782	.786
Apr	.735	.741	.740	.736	.744	.751	.750	.747	.751
May	.723	.729	.727	.724	.731	.738	.737	.735	.738
Jun	.718	.724	.723	.719	.726	.734	.732	.730	.734
Jul	.717	.723	.722	.718	.726	.733	.732	.729	.733
Aug	.717	.723	.722	.718	.725	.733	.731	.729	.733
Sept	.718	.724	.723	.719	.726	.734	.732	.730	.734
Oct	.709	.715	.714	.711	.718	.725	.724	.721	.725
Nov	.701	.707	.706	.702	.709	.717	.715	.713	.717
Dec	.704	.710	.709	.705	.713	.720	.719	.716	.720
1983									
Jan	.702	.708	.707	.703	.710	.718	.716	.714	.718
Feb	.695	.701	.699	.696	.703	.710	.709	.707	.710
Mar	.692	.698	.696	.693	.700	.707	.706	.704	.707
Apr	.668	.674	.673	.669	.676	.684	.682	.680	.684
May	.661	.667	.666	.662	.669	.677	.675	.673	.677
Jun	.657	.663	.662	.658	.665	.673	.671	.669	.673
Jul	.648	.654	.653	.650	.657	.664	.662	.660	.664
Aug	.641	.647	.646	.642	.649	.656	.655	.653	.656
Sept	.634	.640	.638	.635	.642	.649	.648	.645	.649
Oct	.628	.634	.633	.629	.636	.643	.642	.640	.643
Nov	.622	.628	.627	.623	.630	.637	.636	.634	.637
Dec	.618	.624	.623	.619	.626	.633	.632	.630	.633
1984									
Jan	.619	.625	.624	.620	.627	.634	.633	.631	.634
Feb	.612	.618	.617	.614	.620	.627	.626	.624	.627
Mar	.607	.613	.612	.608	.615	.622	.621	.619	.622
Apr	.586	.592	.591	.587	.594	.601	.600	.597	.601
May	.580	.586	.585	.581	.588	.595	.594	.591	.595
Jun	.576	.582	.581	.577	.584	.591	.590	.587	.591
Jul	.578	.584	.582	.579	.586	.593	.591	.589	.593
Aug	.563	.569	.568	.564	.571	.578	.577	.574	.578
Sept	.560	.566	.565	.561	.568	.575	.574	.571	.575
Oct	.551	.556	.555	.552	.558	.565	.564	.562	.565
Nov	.546	.551	.550	.547	.554	.560	.559	.557	.560
Dec	.547	.553	.552	.548	.555	.561	.560	.558	.561
1985									
Jan	.542	.547	.546	.543	.549	.556	.555	.553	.556
Feb	.529	.535	.534	.530	.537	.543	.542	.540	.543
Mar	.515	.520	.519	.516	.523	.529	.528	.526	.529
Apr	.483	.489	.488	.485	.491	.497	.496	.494	.497
May	.477	.482	.481	.478	.484	.490	.489	.487	.490
Jun	.474	.479	.478	.475	.481	.487	.486	.484	.487
Jul	.476	.482	.481	.477	.484	.490	.489	.487	.490
Aug	.472	.478	.477	.473	.480	.486	.485	.483	.486
Sept	.473	.478	.477	.474	.481	.487	.486	.484	.487
Oct	.471	.476	.475	.472	.478	.484	.483	.481	.484

Starting month for Indexation	Apr	May	Jun	Jul	Aug	Sept	Oct	Nov	Dec
Nov	.466	.471	.470	.467	.473	.479	.478	.476	.479
Dec	.464	.469	.468	.465	.471	.477	.476	.474	.477

Month of disposal 1993

1986

	Apr	May	Jun	Jul	Aug	Sept	Oct	Nov	Dec
Jan	.461	.466	.465	.462	.468	.474	.473	.471	.474
Feb	.455	.461	.460	.456	.463	.469	.468	.466	.469
Mar	.454	.459	.458	.455	.461	.467	.466	.464	.467
Apr	.440	.445	.444	.441	.447	.453	.452	.450	.453
May	.437	.442	.441	.438	.444	.450	.449	.447	.450
Jun	.438	.443	.442	.439	.445	.451	.450	.448	.451
Jul	.442	.447	.446	.443	.449	.455	.454	.523	.455
Aug	.437	.442	.441	.438	.444	.451	.450	.448	.451
Sept	.430	.435	.434	.431	.437	.444	.442	.440	.444
Oct	.428	.433	.432	.429	.435	.441	.440	.438	.441
Nov	.416	.421	.420	.417	.423	.429	.428	.426	.429
Dec	.411	.416	.415	.412	.418	.424	.423	.421	.424

1987

	Apr	May	Jun	Jul	Aug	Sept	Oct	Nov	Dec
Jan	.406	.411	.410	.407	.413	.419	.418	.416	.419
Feb	.400	.405	.404	.401	.407	.413	.412	.410	.413
Mar	.398	.403	.402	.399	.405	.411	.410	.408	.411
Apr	.381	.386	.385	.382	.388	.394	.393	.391	.394
May	.380	.385	.384	.381	.387	.393	.392	.390	.393
Jun	.380	.385	.384	.381	.387	.393	.392	.390	.393
Jul	.381	.386	.385	.382	.388	.394	.393	.391	.394
Aug	.377	.382	.381	.378	.384	.390	.389	.387	.390
Sept	.373	.378	.377	.374	.380	.386	.385	.383	.386
Oct	.366	.371	.370	.367	.373	.379	.378	.376	.379
Nov	.360	.365	.364	.361	.367	.372	.371	.369	.372
Dec	.361	.366	.365	.362	.368	.374	.373	.371	.374

1988

	Apr	May	Jun	Jul	Aug	Sept	Oct	Nov	Dec
Jan	.361	.366	.365	.362	.368	.374	.373	.371	.374
Feb	.356	.361	.360	.357	.363	.368	.367	.365	.368
Mar	.351	.355	.354	.352	.357	.363	.362	.360	.363
Apr	.329	.334	.333	.330	.336	.341	.340	.338	.341
May	.324	.329	.328	.325	.331	.336	.335	.333	.336
Jun	.319	.324	.323	.320	.326	.331	.330	.328	.331
Jul	.318	.322	.321	.319	.324	.330	.329	.327	.330
Aug	.303	.308	.307	.304	.310	.315	.314	.312	.315
Sept	.297	.302	.301	.298	.304	.309	.308	.306	.309
Oct	.284	.289	.288	.285	.290	.296	.295	.293	.296
Nov	.278	.283	.282	.279	.285	.290	.289	.287	.290
Dec	.275	.279	.278	.276	.281	.286	.286	.284	.286

1989

	Apr	May	Jun	Jul	Aug	Sept	Oct	Nov	Dec
Jan	.267	.271	.270	.268	.273	.278	.277	.276	.278
Feb	.258	.262	.261	.258	.264	.269	.268	.267	.269
Mar	.252	.256	.256	.253	.258	.264	.263	.261	.264
Apr	.230	.234	.234	.231	.236	.241	.241	.239	.241
May	.223	.227	.226	.223	.229	.234	.233	.231	.234
Jun	.218	.223	.222	.219	.224	.230	.229	.227	.230
Jul	.217	.222	.221	.218	.223	.229	.228	.226	.229
Aug	.214	.218	.218	.215	.220	.225	.225	.223	.225
Sept	.206	.210	.209	.207	.212	.217	.216	.214	.217

Starting month for Indexation	Apr	May	Jun	Jul	Aug	Sept	Oct	Nov	Dec
Oct	.197	.201	.200	.197	.203	.208	.207	.205	.208
Nov	.186	.191	.190	.187	.192	.197	.197	.195	.197
Dec	.184	.188	.187	.184	.189	.194	.194	.192	.194

Month of disposal 1993

1990
	Apr	May	Jun	Jul	Aug	Sept	Oct	Nov	Dec
Jan	.177	.181	.180	.177	.182	.187	.187	.185	.187
Feb	.170	.174	.173	.171	.176	.181	.180	.178	.181
Mar	.158	.162	.161	.159	.164	.169	.168	.166	.169
Apr	.124	.128	.127	.125	.129	.134	.133	.132	.134
May	.114	.118	.117	.115	.120	.124	.124	.122	.124
Jun	.110	.114	.113	.110	.115	.120	.119	.118	.120
Jul	.109	.113	.112	.110	.114	.119	.118	.117	.119
Aug	.098	.101	.101	.098	.103	.108	.107	.105	.108
Sept	.087	.091	.090	.088	.093	.097	.097	.095	.097
Oct	.079	.083	.082	.080	.084	.089	.088	.087	.089
Nov	.082	.085	.085	.082	.087	.092	.091	.089	.092
Dec	.082	.086	.085	.083	.088	.092	.092	.090	.092

1991
	Apr	May	Jun	Jul	Aug	Sept	Oct	Nov	Dec
Jan	.080	.084	.083	.081	.085	.090	.089	.088	.090
Feb	.074	.078	.077	.075	.079	.084	.083	.082	.084
Mar	.070	.074	.073	.071	.075	.080	.079	.078	.080
Apr	.056	.060	.059	.057	.062	.066	.065	.064	.066
May	.053	.057	.056	.054	.058	.063	.062	.061	.063
Jun	.048	.052	.051	.049	.054	.058	.057	.056	.058
Jul	.051	.055	.054	.052	.056	.061	.060	.058	.061
Aug	.048	.052	.051	.049	.054	.058	.057	.056	.058
Sept	.045	.048	.048	.045	.050	.054	.053	.052	.054
Oct	.041	.044	.044	.041	.046	.050	.050	.048	.050
Nov	.037	.041	.040	.038	.042	.046	.046	.044	.046
Dec	.036	.040	.039	.037	.041	.046	.045	.043	.046

1992
	Apr	May	Jun	Jul	Aug	Sept	Oct	Nov	Dec
Jan	.037	.041	.040	.038	.042	.046	.046	.044	.046
Feb	.032	.035	.034	.032	.037	.041	.040	.039	.041
Mar	.029	.032	.031	.029	.034	.038	.037	.036	.038
Apr	.013	.017	.016	.014	.018	.022	.022	.020	.022
May	.009	.013	.012	.010	.014	.019	.018	.017	.019
Jun	.009	.013	.012	.010	.014	.019	.018	.017	.019
Jul	.013	.017	.016	.014	.018	.022	.022	.020	.022
Aug	.012	.016	.015	.013	.017	.022	.021	.019	.022
Sept	.009	.012	.011	.009	.014	.018	.017	.016	.018
Oct	.005	.009	.008	.006	.010	.014	.014	.012	.014
Nov	.006	.010	.009	.007	.011	.016	.015	.014	.016
Dec	.010	.014	.013	.011	.015	.019	.019	.017	.019

1993
	Apr	May	Jun	Jul	Aug	Sept	Oct	Nov	Dec
Jan	.020	.023	.022	.020	.025	.029	.028	.027	.029
Feb	.013	.017	.016	.014	.018	.022	.022	.020	.022
Mar	.009	.013	.012	.010	.014	.019	.018	.017	.019
Apr		.004	.003	.001	.005	.009	.009	.007	.009
May			Nil	Nil	.001	.006	.005	.004	.006
Jun				Nil	.002	.006	.006	.004	.006
Jul					.004	.009	.008	.006	.009
Aug						.004	.004	.002	.004
Sept							Nil	Nil	Nil
Oct								Nil	.001
Nov									.002
Dec									

TABLE 6

SOCIAL SECURITY BENEFITS

Taxable

Income Support (1)
Industrial Death Benefit Pensions
Invalid Care Allowance (2)
Retirement Pension (2)
Statutory Maternity Pay
Statutory Sick Pay
Unemployment Benefit (2)
Widowed Mother's Allowance
Widow's Pension

Non-taxable

Sickness Benefit
Maternity Allowance
Child Benefit
Child's Special Allowance
Industrial Disablement Benefit
Severe Disablement Allowance
Invalidity Benefit (3)
Disability Working Allowance
Widow's Payment
Family Credit
Guardian's Allowance
Housing Benefit
Income Support (1)
One-Parent Benefit
War Widow's Pension
Social Fund Payments
Attendance Allowance

Notes

(1) Income Support is taxable when paid to the unemployed who 'sign on', or to those on strike.

(2) Child dependent additions to these benefits are not taxable.

(3) Invalidity Benefit will be brought into tax at a suitable opportunity.

1993 BUDGET MEASURES

In the first Autumn Budget the Chancellor of the Exchequer, Mr. Clarke, announced last November that the main personal allowances will be held at their current levels for 1994/95. The statutory requirement to compensate for inflation will be overridden. Nor are any changes proposed to the lower, basic and higher rates of tax which remain at 20%, 25% and 40% respectively.

As foreshadowed in the March 1993 Budget, the married couple's age allowances are increased by £200 for 1994/95. For 1995/96 they are set to go up by £330. The 20% lower rate band on the first slice of taxable income goes up by £500 to £3,000 for 1994/95. From 6 April 1994 the blind person's allowance increases by £120 to £1,200.

The restriction in the value of the married couple's allowance, and other linked allowances and reliefs, will be implemented for employees by reducing their PAYE tax codes. Codes for 1994/95, incorporating these restrictions, have already been issued.

1994/95 Personal allowances

		£
Personal		3,445
Married couple's		*1,720
Additional personal		*1,720
Age – personal	(age 65-74)	4,200
married couple's	(age 65-74)	*2,665
personal	(age 75 and over)	4,370
married couple's	(age 75 and over)	*2,705
Income limit for age allowance		14,200
Widow's bereavement		*1,720
Relief for blind person (each)		1,200

* Indicates allowances where tax relief is restricted to 20%

Tax rates and bands for 1994/95

Band of Taxable Income	Rate of Tax	Tax on Band	Cumulative Tax
£	%	£	£
0 – 3,000	20	600	600
3,001 – 23,700	25	5,175	5,775
over 23,700	40		

Rates of National Insurance Contributions for 1994/95

CLASS 1 Contributions for Employees

		Standard Rate		Contracted Out	
		On First £57.00	On Remainder	On First £57.00	On Remainder
Contributions levied on all weekly earnings if they reach but do not exceed	£57.00 £430.00	2%	10%	2%	8.2%
If weekly earnings exceed	£430.00	No Additional Contributions		No Additional Contributions	

Reduced Rate for Married Women and Widows with a Valid Election Certificate	3.85%

	£
Men over 65 and Women over 60	Nil
Lower Earnings Limit – Weekly	57
– Monthly	247
– Annually	2,964
Upper Earnings Limit – Weekly	430
– Monthly	1,863
– Annually	22,360

CLASS 2 for Self-Employed

Weekly flat rate	5.65
Small earnings exception	3,200

CLASS 3 Voluntary Contributions

Weekly rate	5.55

CLASS 4 Contributions for the Self-Employed

7.3% of profits between £6,490 and £22,360

Mortgage interest relief

The overall limit on borrowings for the purchase of the borrower's home up to which the interest is eligible for tax relief is unchanged at £30,000. However, from 6 April 1994, the rate of tax relief on mortgage interest paid is restricted to 20% for all taxpayers. At the same time the rules for taxing loans provided by employers will be changed to reduce to 20% the special tax relief on the benefit of cheap or interest-free home loans up to £30,000. The rate of tax relief on interest paid on certain loans used for the purchase of life annuities by elderly people will not be affected. They will continue to receive tax relief at the basic rate.

Maintenance payments

Under Court Orders and Maintenance Agreements made on or after 15 March 1988, the maximum limit on maintenance payments qualifying for tax relief is equivalent to the married couple's allowance. For 1994/95 this limit remains at £1,720. However, like mortgage interest tax relief, the rate of tax relief is now restricted to 20%.

Private medical insurance

An individual who pays private medical insurance premiums for someone aged 60 or over receives tax relief on the premiums providing certain conditions are met. From 6 April 1994 the rate of tax relief will be limited to the basic rate of 25%. This relief will be given wholly by deduction from the amount of the premium due. Higher rate taxpayers will no longer be able to claim any additional reduction in their tax liabilities.

Company cars

A new system, based on the price of a car, comes into effect for taxing company cars. It applies to existing cars still available after 5 April 1994 and to cars newly provided after that date.

The car benefit charge is 35% of the list price of the car. It is reduced by one-third where you do between 2,500 and 17,999 miles a year on business. If your business mileage comes to 18,000 or more the reduction increases to two-thirds. The car benefit is even less for cars which are four or more years old at the end of a tax year. There is then a further reduction of one-third after business mileage has been taken into account.

Illustration

A car was first registered in August 1988. The list price at the time was £9,500. An employee does 13,000 miles on business during the tax year. The taxable benefit amounts to £1,478 calculated as follows:

	£
Car benefit: 35% of list price	3,325
Deduction for business mileage: one-third	1,108
	2,217
Less: Reduction for age of car: one-third	739
Taxable Benefit	£1,478

The 2,500 and 18,000 mileage limits are proportionately reduced if your company car is not available to you for the full tax year. No discounts are given on second cars unless you do at least 18,000 miles on business in that car. The reduction is then one-third.

Any contribution, up to a maximum amount of £5,000, you make towards the purchase price of the car or accessories reduces the list price on which the taxable benefit is calculated.

Illustration
The list price of an employee's new company car is £14,200. He contributes an amount of £3,200 towards the purchase. The price of the car for tax purposes is £11,000.

For the purpose of these new rules the list price of a car will usually be the total of:

- Manufacturer's, importer's or distributor's list price of the car on the day before the date of registration
- Taxes, excluding the Road Fund Licence
- Delivery charges, including VAT
- The list price of any accessory fitted before the car is made available to an employee, including VAT and any delivery or fitting charges
- The list price of any accessory or set of accessories (for example alloy wheels) over £100 (including VAT, fitting and delivery) fitted after the car is made available to an employee. This only applies for accessories fitted after 31 July 1993. Where the price of an employee's car is increased for accessories fitted after the car was made available to him, the increased price applies from the beginning of the tax year in which they were fitted and subsequent years.

There is an upper limit of £80,000 on the price of a car for the purpose of calculating the taxable benefit. Where the list price of a car exceeds this figure, the price for tax purposes will be £80,000.

Company car fuel

The rates of scale benefit for fuel provided for private motoring in company cars are increased by 6% from 6 April 1994. The rates which will apply for 1994/95 are:

	Engine Size cc	Fuel Benefit £
Petrol	0–1400	640
	1401–2000	810
	over 2000	1,200
Diesel	0–2000	580
	over 2000	750

Benefits-in-Kind: loans provided by employers

Cheap or interest-free loans provided by employers are taxable as a benefit-in-kind on directors or employees whose earnings amount to more than £8,500 a year. From 6 April 1994 it is proposed to change the tax treatment of these loans.

Loans which employers provide to employees on the same terms as loans they make to the public will be exempt. The rules for taxing this benefit will be altered to give effect to the restriction in mortgage interest relief. A lower 'official rate' of interest for taxing loans in a foreign currency, where interest rates in that country are significantly lower than interest rates in the UK, will be introduced. At present employer-provided loans are not taxed where the benefit does not exceed £300. A new exemption will be introduced for small loans. It will apply where

- All the employee's cheap or interest-free loans total no more than £5,000 or
- All the employee's cheap or interest-free loans, excluding loans which qualify for tax relief, total no more than £5,000.

Pension schemes earnings limit

Pension contributions for members of occupational pension schemes established on or after 14 March 1989, and for members joining schemes established before that date on or after 1 June 1989, are restricted to those based on a maximum annual earnings limit. This earnings cap is increased from £75,000 to £76,800 from 6 April 1994. It also applies to all Personal Pension Schemes.

Personal Pension Scheme annuities

At present the deduction for Income Tax from each instalment of annuities paid by Approved Personal Pension Schemes is at the 25% basic rate of Income Tax. The Chancellor proposes to bring annuities from personal pension schemes within the Pay As You Earn (PAYE) system. The correct amount of tax, based on each individual's circumstances, will then be deducted from each annuity payment. This change will apply in general to annuities paid after 6 April 1995.

Employees from overseas working in the UK

The Chancellor proposes to ensure that tax will continue to be collected under PAYE from certain groups of employees coming from overseas to work in the United Kingdom. Where only part of the salary is liable to Income Tax, or where it is paid from abroad, the proposals will remove any doubt that tax must be deducted under Pay As Your Earn (PAYE) in these circumstances. This is to prevent the loss to the Exchequer which might arise if employers no longer deducted PAYE. The proposed changes will apply retrospectively to confirm that PAYE has been operated properly in the past and will continue to operate in the same way in the future.

Value Added Tax

From the start of their next accounting period after 6 April 1994, businesses must use the new scale charges for motor fuel as shown in the following table:

	Diesel		Petrol	
Car cc	Scale Charge £	VAT £	Scale Charge £	VAT £
1400 or less	145	21.60	160	23.83
1401–1999	145	21.60	202	30.09
2000 or more	187	27.85	300	44.68